PENGUIN  CLASSICS

THE ROMANCE OF TRISTAN

Nothing at all is known about BEROUL, one of the earliest poets to treat the *Tristan* legend. He wrote in about the middle of the twelfth century.

•

ALAN S. FEDRICK, M.A., PH.D., was born in Plymouth in 1937, and was educated at Lincoln College, Oxford, and Manchester University. He was lecturer at London University from 1963 until 1968 and subsequently Professor of Comparative Literature at Brandeis University, Massachusetts. His interest in the *Tristan* romances began during his undergraduate days at Oxford, and he published several articles on aspects of the legend. Alan Fedrick died in 1975.

THE ROMANCE OF

TRISTAN

by Beroul

AND

THE TALE OF
TRISTAN'S MADNESS

•

TRANSLATED TOGETHER
FOR THE FIRST TIME
by Alan S. Fedrick

PENGUIN BOOKS

PENGUIN BOOKS

Published by the Penguin Group
Penguin Books Ltd, 80 Strand, London WC2R 0RL, England
Penguin Putnam Inc., 375 Hudson Street, New York, New York 10014, USA
Penguin Books Australia Ltd, 250 Camberwell Road, Camberwell, Victoria 3124, Australia
Penguin Books Canada Ltd, 10 Alcorn Avenue, Toronto, Ontario, Canada M4V 3B2
Penguin Books India (P) Ltd, 11 Community Centre, Panchsheel Park, New Delhi – 110 017, India
Penguin Books (NZ) Ltd, Cnr Rosedale and Airborne Roads, Albany, Auckland, New Zealand
Penguin Books (South Africa) (Pty) Ltd, 24 Sturdee Avenue, Rosebank 2196, South Africa

Penguin Books Ltd, Registered Offices: 80 Strand, London WC2R 0RL, England

www.penguin.com

This translation first published 1970

041

**Copyright © Alan S. Fedrick, 1970
All rights reserved**

Printed and bound in Great Britain by Clays Ltd, Elcograf S.p.A.
Filmset in Monotype Ehrhardt

ISBN-13: 978–0–140–44230–4

www.greenpenguin.co.uk

MIX
Paper from
responsible sources
FSC® C018179

Penguin Books is committed to a sustainable
future for our business, our readers and our planet.
This book is made from Forest Stewardship
Council™ certified paper.

To My Parents

CONTENTS

THE ROMANCE OF TRISTAN

INTRODUCTION

BEROUL'S POEM

TRISTAN and Yseut are not the only pair of tragic lovers the world has known, and they were certainly not the first. Yet this tragic tale of love, more than any other, has succeeded in capturing men's imagination from the time when it first appeared in the twelfth century. For eight centuries it has been the inspiration of countless story-tellers, poets, dramatists, painters, sculptors and composers. The unique fascination of the Tristan legend seems to lie not in the accretions which have been added to it with the passage of time, however firmly attached to the Tristan legend these have become, but rather in the unadorned central theme: the unsought passion which draws Tristan and Yseut irresistibly together at a time when the memory of Tristan slaying Yseut's uncle in combat is still fresh in their minds, and which compels them later to cut across the moral code and the social and family obligations which are the framework of their existence. Because of their passion they undergo a range of suffering through moral guilt, social degradation, and material hardships of all kinds until at last the anguish of separation is forced on them. Tristan's unhappy life reaches a new intensity of grief when he is falsely told, as he lies desperately ill in Brittany, that his beloved Yseut has not answered his last plea and come from Cornwall to see him; his spirit can stand no more, and

9

he dies thinking that his loved one has failed him at the last.

The mystery which surrounds the cause of all this suffering, the love potion, is undeniably an essential part of the legend's fascination. In the earliest versions of the story the love potion comes into the narrative suddenly and unexpectedly, and its effect is to bind together two people who have no reason to like each other and whose relations are indeed more hostile than friendly. The potion may well have been originally no more than a narrative device which supplied the mainspring of the story, but later adaptors, from Gottfried von Strassburg in the thirteenth century to Richard Wagner in the nineteenth, endowed it with immense symbolic value. The theme of the love potion is probably the best-known distinguishing feature of the Tristan legend, and it is in their attitude to this theme that later authors differ most widely. This is perhaps partly because in the very earliest poems the love potion is presented by the narrator with a complete absence of explanatory comment; so much is left unsaid that later authors are, as it were, invited to fill the artistic vacuum surrounding the potion with some sort of elucidation. But in Beroul's poem we have not yet arrived at the 'explanatory' stage of narrative fiction, and Beroul's treatment of the potion theme is discussed below.

There are in existence now hundreds of different versions of the Tristan legend, written in practically every European language, and the majority of them reflect an individual interpretation of the legend and treatment of its basic themes. In the early years of this century an epoch-making discovery was made by the great French scholar, Joseph Bédier: in the course of his studies of the Tristan legend, he found that all Tristan poems now known, medieval and modern, can be traced back to a single poem, now lost, which is the fountain-head of the whole tradition and the archetype of all Tristan stories.* Amongst all the extant romances, Beroul's *Tristan* has a special claim on our attention not merely because it happens to be the oldest but because it comes closest to preserving what may be called the raw material of the legend.† Most of the unexplained and mysterious events of the story, which contributed so greatly to its fascination for later ages, are found in Beroul's poem, and Beroul presents them just as they are without any attempt

* J. Bédier, *Le Roman de Tristan par Thomas* (Paris, 1902, 1905) vol. II, introduction. Bédier's argument may be briefly summarized as follows: he showed first that all known Tristan stories could be traced back either to the twelfth century poems of Eilhart von Oberg or Thomas d'Angleterre, or to the thirteenth-century French prose romance: the only exceptions were the poem of Beroul and the short tale of Tristan's madness, both translated here. There were therefore five so-called primary versions of the legend, none of which appeared to be the derivative of any other. At the same time, Bédier showed that these five versions concur in presenting the majority of the central episodes in the same order in the narrative. The striking fact which emerged from his comparison of the five stories was not the multiplicity of different episodes, but their rarity. In good logic, it must follow that the five primary versions are themselves the derivatives of a single poem, although Bédier did not ignore the possibility of any number of intermediaries.

Bédier's theory of the Tristan archetype is now generally accepted by scholars.

† The beginning and end of Beroul's poem have not been preserved. In order to present a complete story in this book, summaries of missing episodes have been included as well as a translation of the tale of Tristan's madness, which fills an important gap in the later stages.

at explanation. In reading Beroul's poem we are not only transported into the medieval setting for a tale of tragic love, but we are confronted with a conception of the story-teller's art which is foreign to our own. Partly for this reason, Beroul's poem contains much that will startle and baffle a present-day reader who judges it by the modern aesthetic criteria of fictional narratives. There is no doubt that Beroul's poem is sadly defective by modern standards; for it is far from easy to imagine that a piece of narrative fiction can exist as a serious work of art while dispensing with elements as fundamental as a coherent plot, an ordered flow of events with a clearly discernible causal nexus, and convincing characterization. Narratives of that kind existed nevertheless at a stage in the history of literature which is still only imperfectly understood, in the 'pre-literary' period before our present-day aesthetic began to be formed, when romances were designed for oral recitation and when men knew no better than to believe what they saw and heard. It is as a representative of this earlier aesthetic* that Beroul's poem is to be judged, not as a quaint and clumsy attempt to write a story according to modern literary criteria. Before dealing with some of the strange features of Beroul's poem, however, there is a problem which merits a brief preliminary consideration, namely the authorship of the poem.†

* My own ideas on this topic were for the most part inspired by a brilliant lecture given by E. Vinaver in 1963, entitled 'Epic to Romance', since published in *The Bulletin of the John Rylands Library*.

† I have stated above that Beroul's poem is the oldest of the *Tristan* romances, although I am aware that this is far from universally accepted. My reasons for this should be clear from the rest of the introduction and I do not propose to examine the question of dating as a separate issue.

The single manuscript of Beroul's *Tristan* is faulty
in several respects and wholly unworthy of the poem.*
The text has been much studied and the puzzles it
presents are the centre of controversy amongst scholars.
In an effort to solve some of the literary problems a
number of ingenious theories have been evolved con-
cerning the actual composition of the manuscript. It has
been suggested that the manuscript is in fact riddled
with interpolations; and philological experts have
claimed to detect features showing that the early part of
the poem was written by a different author from the
later. The philological evidence adduced looks extremely
convincing, although I am not sufficiently well-informed
to pass opinion. However, it is obvious that theories of
multiple authorship or heterogeneous composition leave
the literary problems of the text intact. The mere fact
that controversy over the authorship exists, with scholars
of international distinction on both sides, suggests
strongly that there is little to be lost by simply taking
the text as it stands. It does not require a trained
scholar to point out the oddities of this poem, and
the philologists' theories have only brought confusion
worse confounded. Let us begin instead with what we

* The manuscript is preserved in the Bibliothèque Nationale in Paris,
MS. B.N. fr. 2171. In preparing this translation I have used the edition
by A. Ewert: *Beroul's Romance of Tristan* (Oxford, 1938); most of the
following remarks on the manuscript are based on Ewert's introduction.
The writing is not elegant, and it is clear that the scribe was careless on
many occasions: the use of capitals and large initials is irregular and does
not necessarily correspond to a division in the narrative; both single
lines and couplets are sometimes omitted, while other lines or parts of
lines are written twice; and several of the letters are not easily distin-
guishable. There appears, however, to be no doubt that it is the work of
a single scribe.

know: I do not think the fact is contested that one man was responsible for the romance as it is now preserved in the manuscript; behind him there may have been dozens of unknown contributors, but there is no doubting the reality of what we may call the man behind the manuscript. This shadowy figure may have been in reality a humble scribe, acting for whatever mundane practical reasons and utterly ignorant of the literary implications of what he did, nonetheless one man composed what is now preserved in that manuscript. Our concern here is with the poem as a piece of literature: we should tackle its problems in literary terms without making *a priori* assumptions of its faulty transmission. If elements of doubt subsist, let us give the benefit to Beroul* by granting that the poem which was actually written was also the poem he meant to write.

We may pass without further preamble to some of the strange features of Beroul's poem, beginning with a consideration of the poet's techniques of characterization. It is immediately apparent that at least one aspect is different from modern practice, namely the complete absence of what Jean Genet has called, in a perceptive phrase, 'the author's politeness towards the reader', signifying that the author does not seek to impose his own judgements. Thus, an author who wished to portray a virtuous character would not now be content with stating that this character is virtuous: on the contrary, he would present a character who thought virtuously and acted

---

* For the sake of convenience I shall use Beroul as the poet's name although this is also a matter of doubt.

virtuously; it would then be up to the reader to draw his own conclusions, or if the author did pronounce an explicit judgement there would at least be no question of the reader disagreeing. This will doubtless seem too obvious to be worth saying; but the curious thing is that Beroul's technique is quite different. In the manner of the poets of the Old French epic poems, the *chansons de geste*, Beroul never argues the case for his characters: in Genet's sense, Beroul is far from 'polite', for he constantly intervenes in the narrative to proclaim his sympathy for the lovers and his hostility to their enemies. But there is more to this than the question of whether or not the author makes his sympathies known, for Beroul's expressed opinions are at times not wholly borne out by the facts he presents.

A brief example will illustrate this point: at the court of King Mark there are three barons, almost always described as 'the three villains', who are both cowardly and jealous of Tristan's prowess. When they are introduced at the beginning of the episode in which they try to trap Tristan the narrator says (p. 60): 'You never saw more wicked men!' The narrator goes on not, as we might have expected, to speak of the fearful crimes these men had committed, but to say that they were resolved to ask King Mark to banish Tristan. Their reason for this was that they had seen Tristan with Yseut in situations that were evidently compromising (p. 60), and specifically lying together naked in the king's bed several times. Now, nothing could be more reasonable or loyal than the barons' resolve, without taking their motives into account: the fidelity of the king's wife was essential both for the king's honour and to ensure the unquestioned succession of his heirs to his lands and titles; and Mark had taken a wife for the explicit purpose of begetting heirs. The barons' behaviour in this respect does not seem to be objectionable and it hardly justifies the poet's opinion. The barons suggest to Mark a stratagem by which he can find out for himself the truth of their accusations, and they take into their counsel a dwarf who is a magician. This action is somewhat underhand out of necessity, although it is excusable in terms of protecting the king's honour. But when the dwarf comes on the scene (p. 61), what a flood of invective the poet hurls at him! Dwarfs in medieval romance are traditionally evil creatures, and Frocin was no exception. Even so, the poet's strong language is hardly borne out by what follows, for the dwarf merely suggests an ingenious means of proving to the king that Tristan and Yseut are in fact lovers – a means, moreover, which is very nearly successful. To counterbalance the poet's attitude, it should be stressed that it was imperative for the king to know if his wife was unfaithful, hence that even clandestine attempts to prove this were justifiable, not to say laudable. Nonetheless, the poet persists in heaping abuse on the dwarf and on the three barons until each of them meets his death. I hold no brief for the three barons, but the issue of their villainy is certainly less clear-cut than the poet's attitude suggests; at the same time, the themes of their cowardice and their jealousy of Tristan are sufficiently prominent for us not to be shocked by the arbitrariness of the poet's hostility. But the poet's attitude to these men who were acting in the king's interest bespeaks a strong prejudice: what are we to make of this prejudice?

One answer that can readily be given is that the poet has great sympathy for Tristan and Yseut whatever happens, hence a corresponding dislike of their enemies regardless of the grounds of their antagonism. In this way the barons' villainy is a function of their hostility to Tristan. The three barons are not villains so much because of what they do as because the poet says they are; for whatever action they take is presented as a piece of villainy. At this point we begin to glimpse a surprising and significant aspect of Beroul's aesthetic, which depends on nothing less than an unquestioning acceptance of the narrator's attitudes. We shall return to this point later. Meanwhile, let us consider for a moment the other side of the narrator's hostility to the three barons, to see whether the lovers really merit the sympathy he has for them.

We are told countless times that Yseut is noble, wise and fair and that Tristan is noble, brave and strong; but a certain amount of explanation is needed, for it must be admitted that they do not always act in a way that is noticeably noble or wise. As a pair of lovers indulging in an adulterous passion, their conduct is apparently *de facto* reprehensible without further discussion. On the other hand, if the love potion is considered to be at once the cause and the justification of their passion, it relieves them of responsibility for their crime (see below pp. 20–24). Even if the potion does excuse their passion, however, it is still difficult at times to see how it can excuse what seem to be the lovers' attitudes to their illicit love. The scene at which the Beroul manuscript begins offers a case in point, for Yseut is seen less as the archetype of a noble suffering lover than as one of those cunning and deceitful wives familiar in the pages of the *Decameron*. When she declares (p. 48) that she has never loved anyone except the man to whom she came as a maiden, she knows that Mark will take this to mean that she has always been faithful to him. It might perhaps be argued at this point that Yseut makes her declaration with the best intentions, that she is seeking to avoid hurting Mark by revealing the truth about her love for Tristan. But such an interpretation would hardly be consistent with the account which Yseut gives later to Brangain pp. 54–5), for Yseut sees it only as a piece of deception successfully carried out, which is going to make things easier for herself and Tristan. Equally, her words to Mark (pp. 55–8) bear out the conclusion that her only object was to deceive the king. If the love potion did compel Yseut to follow a course of action which she did not choose, it is at least plain that she managed to keep all her wits about her.

There is a further factor which needs to be taken into account in considering the lovers' behaviour, for our attitude to Tristan and Yseut is closely bound up with the role which God plays in the story. In discussing this role, which is no less active than it is ambiguous, we should perhaps not take too literally the exclamations uttered by Brangain and Governal at moments after a crisis has passed, when they thank God for performing a miracle on behalf of the lovers. But there are other cases which cannot be glossed over so easily: for example, when Tristan is taken captive by the three barons (p. 65) he is careful to behave correctly and submit to this indignity, for the poet tells us that his trust in God is so great that he knows he will be successful in a judicial combat. The combat Tristan is thinking of would presumably have been on the issue of whether or not he had an illicit love for the queen. Now, Tristan's skill as a warrior is well known, and it is likely that he would not find an opponent; but on what does he base his trust in God?.

Before trying to answer that question two further examples should be considered. In the scene of 'The Tryst under the Tree' Yseut swears 'before God' that she has never loved anyone except the man to whom she came as a maiden. Her words are literally true but, as we have seen, they are spoken in order to deceive the king. A similar and even more blatant piece of deception is the declaration made by Yseut in the presence of King Arthur (p. 142). With her hand stretched over the holy relics she solemnly swears that she has never held any man between her legs except King Mark her husband and the leper 'as everyone who was watching could see'. Once again her words are literally true and at the same time misleading, for once again King Mark is deceived as to her real meaning. The dramatic irony of these two situations is apparent: the first time what Mark takes to be a protestation of her innocence is in reality a re-affirmation of her love for Tristan; and the second time she simply states a fact which has implications that the king is unaware of. Both these statements, however, are made with God as witness. In both cases Mark, not God, is deceived. Are we therefore to conclude, as Gottfried von Strassburg did, that

'Christ in His great virtue is pliant as a windblown sleeve. . . . He is at the beck of every heart for honest deeds or fraud.'* For it is clear that God either connived at the lovers' illicit passion or in some sense considered them innocent. Even if we assume that God's attitude to the lovers is an extension of the narrator's sympathies and that He takes advantage, so to speak, of the literal truth of Yseut's words to let her go unpunished, some sort of justification is still called for.

In 1835 the distinguished French medieval scholar, Paulin Paris, pronounced that the adulterous love of Tristan and Yseut was morally superior to the adulterous love of Lancelot and Guinevere on the grounds that the love potion relieved the former pair of moral responsibility. If this view is accepted, no further explanation of God's mercy is needed. And this is indeed the view that Beroul seems to point to when the lovers tell Friar Ogrin that their love is caused by a magic potion when they meet him accidentally in the forest. This reference to the potion is made during their period of exile in the forest, which is perhaps where they undergo their deepest suffering. A reward has been offered for their capture by Mark, which forces them to be constantly on the move, and they have no food apart from the game killed by Tristan. In the course of their meeting with the hermit Ogrin it is the sinful aspect of their love which is stressed for the first time. Although they can now safely indulge their passion it is only at the expense of every material and spiritual comfort; while they are in the forest they

* Gottfried von Strassburg, *Tristan*, trans. A. T. Hatto (Penguin Classics, Harmondsworth, 1960) p. 248.

live in a state of guilt-edged security. But the poet tells us several times that because of their great love neither felt any hardship.

When the lovers tell Ogrin of the potion, there is of course no reasoned argument; they do not present it as their excuse. Nor do Tristan or Yseut or even Ogrin pause to examine the implications; for this is not the way of the poet. Ogrin simply exhorts them further to repent. But when the lovers come to him later, after the potion's effect has worn off, to seek his advice about returning to Mark, his sympathy for them and his joy are evident, and he does his casuistical best to help them, although Yseut makes it clear that she does not repent and still loves Tristan honourably. Ogrin strengthens the help he is able to give them by making use of Mark's legal error in condemning the lovers wrongly.* But before we can consider the love potion as absolving the lovers from moral responsibility for their passion we shall have to give some consideration to what is perhaps the potion's most surprising attribute, namely that it wears off after three years.

First of all, there is something intrinsically odd about limiting the duration of the love potion's efficacy. Without doubt, Yseut's mother acted wisely and thoughtfully in trying by magical means to ensure affection between her

* Mark was at fault in condemning the lovers summarily, without trial. According to legal codes in France in the twelfth century, an adulterer could be summarily punished only if taken *in flagrante delicto*. Tristan and Yseut were not, of course, so caught, and Mark took their guilt as proved by the circumstantial evidence of the blood in the bed and on the floor. The poet presents this as an important element in justifying the lovers, for it is also mentioned more than once by Tristan himself and by the people of Cornwall.

daughter and the husband she had never seen. But it is difficult to imagine that this thoughtfulness extended to giving back to Yseut the freedom of her affections after three years. However, the potion's limitation is very precisely marked: three years to the day after it was drunk Tristan is out hunting a stag; the exact hour comes back and Tristan immediately stops, apparently caught in mid-stride, and begins to think of the harm he has done to Mark and of the wretchedness of the life in the forest.

The limitation of the potion's efficacy is first mentioned a few lines earlier in the poem without any warning. Although our present-day literary aesthetic discourages this sort of unexpected turn in the narrative, the reason for Beroul's sudden revelation of the potion's limitation is not far to seek. It is of great importance to bear in mind the strikingly episodic structure of the romance, for we have to deal here with two distinct episodes. When the potion is drunk, the important detail is that it has the power to make Tristan and Yseut fall irresistibly in love; at that point it is not a narrative requirement to know that that power is of limited duration. When the potion's efficacy ends, however, the situation in the narrative is more complex, and the story indeed appears to be heading for an abrupt and highly unsatisfactory end. Tristan made a mistake in analysing Mark's motives in leaving recognition tokens behind when he found the lovers asleep in their bower, for he thought Mark had done this only to deceive them and had in fact gone for more men (p. 95). As a consequence, the lovers have taken flight and are crossing the forest of Morrois apparently well on their way to Wales. The story could not continue with Tristan and Yseut safe in Wales while Mark remains in Cornwall. Mark's presence is indispensable for the story and some way has to be found to bring him once more into the same setting as the lovers. While the lovers are under the potion's influence, however, it is unthinkable that they could ever seek a reconciliation with Mark, for that would be hardly compatible with the basic theme of their love.* It is at this point in the narrative that the potion's efficacy comes to an end and the lovers immediately think about returning to Mark. Clearly, the limitation of the potion's efficacy fulfils an urgent requirement in the story. Has it at the same time a deeper significance than that of a narrative device?

The obvious answer is that the love of Tristan and Yseut continues to the end of the romance and does not end when the potion's efficacy ends; without their love there would be no story. The fragment of Beroul's poem opens with Tristan paying a clandestine visit to Yseut in the orchard of Mark's castle; at this time they are under the influence of the potion. Then the potion's efficacy ends, and Yseut announces proudly to Friar Ogrin that she no longer sleeps with Tristan; but the friendship she bears him remains evidently very close, for the fragment stops when Tristan is paying another clandestine visit to Yseut, this time in her bedroom in Mark's castle, while the three barons arrange to spy on 'the sport that Tristan was enjoying'. Furthermore, we

* Nonetheless, in the *Tristan* poem of Thomas d'Angleterre, where the potion's efficacy is lifelong, the lovers do return to court when Mark invites them to. But this does not happen without a serious loss of dignity on the king's part.

may remember the affection in their parting words to each other, indicating that the bonds between them are still strong – an impression borne out by the fact that they do not actually part until after the Beroul fragment ends. There seems to be no doubt that the end of the love potion's efficacy does not correspond to the end of love, illogical as this may be. It follows from this that the limitation is precisely a narrative device which gives a superficial plausibility to the lovers' seeking to end their life in the forest and so return to Mark.

The suggestion that the potion is the lovers' justification can now be seen in a wider perspective. If we accept the truth of Yseut's affirmation to the hermit after the potion wears off, then the nature of her love for Tristan has changed. We learn nothing from the poet which explicitly contradicts the idea that their love has now become blameless, provided only that we discount the suspicions of the three barons. Since a magic potion as the cause of love evidently does absolve the lovers from moral guilt, there is equally no reason that we should not accept Paulin Paris's confident assertion.

The love potion is clearly a great convenience for the story, firstly by removing the moral stain from the lovers' adulterous passion when its influence begins, and secondly by enabling the lovers to return to Mark when its influence stops. In addition, the poet's treatment of the potion theme highlights a principle of his aesthetic which is in sharp contrast to modern notions. To state this simply: before we can begin to appreciate the story in Beroul's terms we have to ignore the impulse to carry over the facts learned in one episode to a second episode.

It may well happen that all the details of a given scene are not relevant in another scene dealing with the same theme; and this is doubtless the explanation, at least in part, for a number of discrepancies and contradictions in the narrative.

It is necessary to insist on this question of episodic structure because Beroul's poem, written in rhyming couplets, has all the appearance of a long continuous narrative; in this respect it contrasts with the older French epic poems, composed in narrative units known as *laisses*, varying in length from a few lines to over a hundred, in which all the lines end with the same assonance or rhyme. Hence these epic poems actually look as if they have an episodic structure. What Beroul did may be broadly described as combining the structure of the epic poems with the verse form of continuous narrative, with the result that his poem may be considered a *chanson de geste* in octosyllabic couplets.

That Beroul's narrative proceeds in a series of episodes is something that can be easily observed and accepted; that this episodic structure is a cornerstone of the aesthetic which underlies the poem is less easy to accept. Where the narrator's attention is concentrated on the single episode, on what M. P. Le Gentil has called 'the impression of the moment', a detail which has its place in one episode may implicitly or explicitly contradict a detail in another episode.

The love potion itself seems to be one example, and this point can be further illustrated. When Mark is re-assured of the lovers' innocence after the scene of 'The Tryst under the Tree', he resolves to have the evil dwarf put to death; the dwarf learns of the king's intention and immediately flees towards Wales. At the beginning of the episode of 'The Flour on the Floor', which follows soon after, the three barons arouse Mark's suspicions again and, to help in devising a means to trap the lovers, send for the dwarf; he has apparently been waiting outside the room, for he comes in quickly (p. 61). The poet tells us neither where the dwarf has come from nor what is Mark's attitude to him. A sharper contradiction appears later in the story when Yseut is returned to Mark, and the three barons advise him not to allow Tristan at his court for a time. Mark accepts this advice, saying that he will always follow their advice, whatever happens (p. 112). But less than a month later, when the same three barons advise Mark to order Yseut to vindicate herself publicly against the accusation of loving Tristan, the king refuses angrily and his wrath is so fierce that the barons retreat in alarm (p. 115).

It is the existence of these and other similar discrepancies which has led to the appearance of a number of different theories of the work's composition, ranging from the serious and recondite to the frankly entertaining. This is not the place to discuss these theories, and I have already suggested that it may not be necessary in approaching Beroul's poem from a purely literary angle. But I will call attention to a strange theory which was advanced a century ago by the German scholar Heinzel. He noted that the poem could be divided into nineteen episodes, some of which contradict each other in some way; he believed he could detect the passages where these episodes had been cobbled together; and in consequence postulated nineteen different authors. Now this is not very good logic: Ockham's razor will shave away most of those nineteen hypothetical figures. Even so, Heinzel's theory holds to my mind a valuable clue to a truer appreciation of Beroul's poem simply by underlining the possibility of a comparable division of the narrative. With the principle of division into episodes we cannot seriously take issue; but in place of Heinzel's interpretation I would advance a much simpler suggestion: that since Beroul's poem exists as a narrative made up by joining together a series of single episodes we should accept this as a legitimate means of telling a story. As the author of Beroul's poem I would propose, not Heinzel's collaboration of bunglers, but one man who knew what he was doing; not nineteen men who failed to produce a story according to our literary standards, but one man who composed a story according to his own standards. I do not mean to imply that contradictions in the narrative, which seem to us to be faults, are in reality virtues according to Beroul's aesthetic; but an assessment of the poem's artistic merit cannot be made until these fundamental differences are known and allowed for.

If the foregoing argument is correct, it follows that Beroul and his audience could enjoy a story, unworried by discrepancies existing between different episodes. This is a crucial point in Beroul's aesthetic, for Beroul's poem is an example of the purely fictional mode of narrative literature.* An essential feature of that mode is that it is unquestioning, in contrast to the so-called

* I am glad to acknowledge here my debt to Northrop Frye's perceptive and stimulating book *The Anatomy of Criticism* (Princeton, 1957).

thematic mode, in which the reader is expected and invited to ponder on the meaning of the material before him. This point may be clarified with an example, and there is in Beroul's poem an excellent illustration of the author's cultivation of the fictional mode as opposed to the thematic. When King Mark comes upon the lovers asleep in the forest and is convinced of their chastity when he sees the sword placed unexpectedly between them (p. 92), it is probably fair to say that the king's surprise is matched by the reader's, for this is an example of one aspect of Beroul's narrative art which is diametrically opposed to our own. The events leading up to the scene which the king witnesses may be briefly retold: Tristan comes back to the bower after hunting a stag; he is tired and wants to sleep. The poet describes with care the positions taken up by the lovers: first he tells us that Tristan placed his sword between their bodies, next that they are fully clothed. This is a strange way for two lovers to go to sleep, and the poet hastens to assure us that their love has not diminished by adding that their arms were round each other and their lips close, although there was a space between them. The poet's comment on this extraordinary situation is most illuminating: he does not say why the lovers were fully clothed, nor why Tristan's sword was placed between them. All that he does say is that if Yseut had been naked that day dreadful harm would have come to them. This comment looks forward to their discovery by Mark; in other words, these remarkable details have their place in the context of the fictional mode, but not the thematic mode.

None of the remarks made in the preceding pages has

a direct bearing on an assessment of the poem's literary merit. I have simply attempted to give a broad outline of the aesthetic framework within which such an assessment can be fairly made. In judging the poem's literary merit we find ourselves on familiar ground, for we need only apply to this poem the standards by which all literature is judged. It is not for me to usurp the reader's function at this point, although I willingly confess to a great liking for the poem.

We cannot, however, praise it unreservedly, and no one would think of claiming that Beroul's poem is without faults. For instance, it is disconcerting to find that the death of one of the three barons in the forest is apparently overlooked in later episodes; no less disconcerting is Tristan's unannounced arrival at some point during Yseut's monologue after the potion has worn off (p. 97); and there are other similar examples. It is also true that Beroul's versification is mediocre, although I would plead that the skill of the poet is sufficient compensation for the clumsiness of the versifier.

It is important to remember that the poem's structure, which requires attention to be concentrated on one episode at a time, does not preclude an overall theme which binds together the different episodes; and this is precisely the role of the theme of tragic love, which runs through the entire poem and gives a sense of unity to the whole. There is consistency, too, in the presentation of the characters, however much we may doubt the narrator's expressed opinions: the villains are always villainous; Governal and Brangain are always loyal; Mark is consistent in his vacillation; and the love of Tristan and Yseut does not waver in intensity, although its nature seems to change.

The narrative itself is full of excitement and swift action, and here the abrupt transitions between episodes are a contributory factor, for the element of surprise is always at hand. The vigorous narration of the lovers' escape from Mark's court (p. 68ff.), with Tristan's sudden and daring leap from the chapel and the quick and violent rescue of Yseut from the lepers' clutches – a scene which includes touches of comedy in the lepers' puffing and panting – offers a good example of the ease with which the story can move rapidly. Suspense is constantly created through ominous remarks by the poet (p. 55): 'The king failed to find his dwarf (God, so much the worse for Tristan!)'; and through the poet's anxious intervention at moments of crisis (p. 63): 'God, why did [Tristan] do this?'

The poet has an undoubted gift for bringing his descriptions to life by his skilful use of telling details. For example, when Mark rushes into his chamber hoping to catch Tristan with Yseut (p. 64) and suspense is at its height, the poet achieves a most unexpected comic effect by telling us suddenly that Tristan was in his own bed pretending to be asleep and snoring loudly. The danger of Tristan's leap from the chapel is emphasized by saying that not even a squirrel could hope to jump down that high cliff and live (p. 68). One further example from many may be quoted, this time a single detail which evokes a whole period of physical hardship for the lovers: when Mark finds the lovers asleep in the forest, he exchanges his ring with Yseut's; formerly the ring had to be forced on but now it slips off easily, so thin have her fingers become. These small but unerring descriptive touches are one of the most admirable features of Beroul's poem, and they may well have been for him a virtually indispensable element of the story-teller's art: bearing in mind that the poem was designed for oral recitation, there is clearly no place for extended descriptions of people or events; hence the special importance of the significant detail.

An unmistakable aspect of Beroul's artistry is his ability to create and sustain humour of all kinds, varying from broad farce to subtle irony. Probably the episode most likely to produce guffaws from the audience is the farcical account of the arrival of all the people of Cornwall at the mud-covered place where Yseut is to vindicate herself (pp. 129–34). Tristan, disguised as a leper, makes a very creditable buffoon and succeeds in getting alms from King Arthur and King Mark as well as making sure that the three barons end up squarely in the marsh – one of them indeed sinks so deep into the mud that only his hair can be seen standing on end. But there is a subtler kind of comedy in Beroul's use of irony. The dramatic irony of Yseut's two false declarations of loyalty to Mark has already been noticed, and the irony of 'The Tryst under the Tree' is recalled in Yseut's conversation with Mark afterwards when she innocently asks the king (p. 57): 'Were you in the pine tree, then, sire?' Mark is again the victim of an ironical combination of circumstances when he discovers the lovers asleep in the forest and is convinced by their chaste attitudes of their innocence (p. 92). Nothing could be further from the truth than Mark's inference on that occasion; and the irony is here pointed up by the episode a few pages before (p. 87) when Governal kills one of the barons and brings his head to show Tristan and Yseut, for when Governal comes into the bower the lovers are tightly clasped in each other's arms, which indicates incidentally that Beroul was not altogether careless about structure.

It may even be suggested that Beroul's whole conception of the story is ironical, for there is an undercurrent of ambiguity running through the poem. The central theme of the love potion is certainly tinged with ambiguity as Beroul presents it: when Tristan and Yseut are on the voyage from Ireland to Cornwall (if we may trust the reconstructed version) they drink a magic potion which causes them to fall instantly in love; at the same time, it is an exceedingly hot day when they drink the potion, their ship is becalmed and the young and handsome pair are separated only by a chess-board. Later in the story, when Tristan correctly submits to being taken captive by the three barons, he expects a judicial combat to be the outcome, and his trust in God is great; at the same time he knows he is the strongest knight at Mark's court, and he later offers to defend Yseut in combat against the accusation of having loved him wrongfully with the knowledge, as Friar Ogrin points out, that no one is likely to oppose him. When the love potion wears off suddenly, both Tristan and Yseut regret the harm they have done King Mark and think of making amends by returning to his court; at the same time, they have been in the forest for a long time, always on the move for fear of being captured, they have been short of food and they have become thin and pale, which is the last detail mentioned by the poet before he announces the potion's limited efficacy (p. 95).

Even from this summary recapitulation of a few events, it does not need a cynic to realize that the whole presentation of the love theme is open to an ambiguous interpretation. It would, however, be falsifying the perspective of Beroul's poem to carry this a stage further and suggest that the story might take place without the love potion and without God's help, for this is not the way Beroul told the story. How much weight should be given to the ambiguities is one of the mysteries of the poem, and it is for each reader to give his own answer. Beroul himself was content to tell the story.

THE TALE OF TRISTAN'S MADNESS

This short anonymous poem relates one of the later episodes in the legend, in which Tristan, disguised as a madman, comes from Brittany to Cornwall to see Yseut, gains entrance to Mark's court, and then tries to get himself recognized by Yseut by making a number of allusions to their past life together. This poem suffers, like Beroul's, from the disadvantage of being preserved in a single, faulty manuscript, and the two poems have a number of practical problems in common as well as certain stylistic similarities.*

* The edition I have used in preparing this translation is that of E. Hoepffner: *La Folie Tristan de Berne* (Paris, 1949). This edition is accompanied by an exhaustive commentary, to which the reader is referred for further information.

This poem seems to have its place in the same aesthetic framework as Beroul's and it would be idle to repeat here remarks already made on that subject. A single example will suffice to illustrate to what extent purely narrative considerations outweigh other factors: when Tristan is speaking to Mark in the presence of Yseut and the whole court (p. 155), he alludes to the time when Mark discovered the lovers asleep in the forest. Now this event could only be known to the three people concerned, and a quicker-thinking Mark would realize that this must be Tristan speaking and would take him captive forthwith. But Mark does not, and we must assume that it was the audacity of this allusion rather than the improbability of Mark's ignoring it that struck the poet's audience.

NOTE ON THE TRANSLATION

Lacunas exist in the manuscripts of both poems. Where possible, the missing words have been supplied on the basis of a comparison with other Tristan poems, and these passages are enclosed in square brackets. The spelling of all names has been regularized and left in the Old French form, except where there is a familiar English form, as Arthur, Gawain. In the original the use of tenses seems to be somewhat capricious: there seemed to be no point in trying to reproduce the wide range of variations and the narrative of this translation is set uniformly in the past.

In general I have tried to strike a balance between a version which is readable in Modern English prose and one which is still recognizably Beroul's poem. All projects of this kind are doomed to fall short in some way or other, perhaps in this case chiefly because stories are no longer told in the way Beroul told his. Some of Beroul's characteristic features I have scarcely attempted to reproduce: the elliptical syntax and occasional parataxis have normally been expanded to bring them into line with modern practice, although I have in principle avoided making Beroul's sentences more complex by introducing subordinating conjunctions where the original has none; and the abruptness of Beroul's style has been somewhat lessened for the sake of clarity.

Many of the best things in Beroul are inevitably lost, but I trust that enough will remain to enable the reader at least to glimpse through the distorting perspective of a translation something of the vigour and artistry of this fine twelfth-century poem.

A. S. F.

ACKNOWLEDGEMENTS

It is first of all a pleasure to thank the co-editor of this series, Robert Baldick, for his constant helpfulness, not to mention a willingness to overlook delays from time to time. For my studies of the *Tristan* romances, and particularly Beroul, I am greatly indebted to the following scholars and friends: J. P. Collas, N. S. Duncan, A. T. Hatto, Elspeth Kennedy, E. Vinaver, F. Whitehead, Gweneth Whitteridge, D. F. Whitton. It goes without saying that if I had listened more carefully to their generously given counsel this book would have been much better, and that only I am to blame for the faults it contains.

In preparing the book for publication I gratefully acknowledge a special debt to two friends at London University: Dafydd Evans, who not only offered many useful suggestions in the course of this work but has always been at hand with friendly advice; and Patricia M. Harry, who read the entire book in typescript and who gave much invaluable help during the period of its preparation.

Finally, I wish to thank Maria Courie, but for whom this book could not have appeared.

Gloucester, Massachusetts   A. S. F.
1969

THE ROMANCE OF
TRISTAN

I

TRISTAN'S BIRTH AND CHILDHOOD*

*Once upon a time, King Mark reigned over Cornwall.
Rivalen, King of Lyoness, learned that Cornwall was being
attacked and crossed the sea to come to Mark's aid. Rivalen
served King Mark so well that as a reward he was given
the hand of Mark's sister, Blanchefleur, with whom he had
fallen in love. They were married in Tintagel, but news of an
attack on his own land immediately recalled Rivalen to
Lyoness. Soon after Rivalen had defeated his enemies
Blanchefleur gave birth to a son, but amid great lamenta-
tion died in childbirth. The child born in sorrow was named
Tristan.*

*Tristan's father entrusted his upbringing to the care of a
wise tutor, Governal, who instructed him in all the warlike
and peaceful arts, as befitted a noble youth. When Tristan
was in his early 'teens, he left his own country with Governal
to seek adventure in other lands. He arrived at the court of
his uncle, King Mark, at Tintagel in Cornwall. He con-
cealed his identity, preferring to serve the king on the same
footing as the other knights-bachelor. But his prowess and
his accomplishments made him stand out above the rest, and
he quickly became a favourite of the king's and was liked
and admired by all the courtiers, especially the king's
Seneschal, Dinas of Lidan. Tristan was soon ready to take
the order of knighthood.*

* This summary of the story before the Beroul fragment begins is
based on J. Bédier's reconstruction of the lost Tristan romance (see
Introduction, p. 11).

MORHOLT OF IRELAND

At this point Mark was suddenly threatened by the arrival at the port of Tintagel of Morholt, brother of the Queen of Ireland, come to demand payment of a tribute owed to Ireland by the Cornish. The tribute consisted of a number of young men and girls to be taken to Ireland as slaves. The grief of the Cornish people was augmented by the cowardly refusal of the barons of Cornwall to face Morholt in single combat to contest his claim to the tribute. Tristan learned of this and decided, after obtaining the approval of his tutor, to undertake the combat himself. Tristan then asked King Mark to knight him; the king agreed, but regretted that it should take place on such an unhappy occasion. Tristan was duly knighted. Messengers from Morholt came to Mark's court and for the last time issued his challenge to meet a knight in single combat. The Cornish barons were again silent, and Tristan offered to do battle with Morholt; Mark was glad to consent to this. However, the Irish messengers declared that Morholt could not fight against an adversary who was not his equal in birth. Tristan then revealed his identity as a king's son and Mark's nephew. Mark was overjoyed at finding his nephew and tried to dissuade him from the dangerous undertaking; but he could not alter Tristan's decision to fight, and the combat was arranged for a few days' time on the Island of St Samson.

On the day fixed, Morholt was first to arrive on the island, where he moored his small boat. Tristan soon followed him, but when he came to the shore and disembarked he pushed his boat out to sea instead of mooring it.

'Why do you do that?' asked Morholt.

'Only one of us will need a boat when this combat is ended,' said Tristan.

Then began the long and fierce combat, watched from the mainland by Mark and his courtiers. Both knights were wounded many times in the struggle, until finally Tristan struck Morholt so hard that the blade of his sword pierced Morholt's helmet and split his skull. The blade broke as Tristan withdrew it, leaving a splinter lodged in Morholt's head. Mortally wounded, Morholt fled to his companions, while Tristan was brought back to land in triumph by Mark and the Cornish. Morholt died on the voyage back to Ireland and his companions were received with great sorrow. Morholt's sister removed the splinter from his cranium and preserved it carefully.

THE MIRACULOUS VOYAGE
FOR HEALING

The wounds Tristan had received in the combat were tended and all were healed save the one from Morholt's poisoned spear. That wound became worse, and a smell began to issue from it which drove everyone away from his bedside, except the faithful Governal. Tristan finally despaired of being cured by human endeavours and resolved, as a last measure, to put his trust in God and set out alone in a boat without sails or oars, in the hope that God would guide him to a place where he might be cured. Mark at first opposed this plan, but eventually gave way and had a boat made ready.

After a sad leave-taking in Cornwall, Tristan set out. He was at sea for many days and nights. At last he neared the coast of a strange country which he soon knew to be Ireland. He began to play his harp and attracted the attention of the Irish king, who came to speak to him. Tristan pretended to be a minstrel called Tantris, on a voyage in a merchant ship which had been attacked by pirates, who had given him a bad wound. The king took Tantris back to his palace where his wound was healed by the medicinal skill of the king's daughter Yseut. Tristan was very much afraid of being recognized in Ireland as the slayer of Morholt and, as soon as he was well enough to travel, he returned to Cornwall.

THE QUEST FOR YSEUT

The barons at Mark's court were making efforts to persuade the king to take a wife, for they were jealous of Tristan and feared that he would gain the inheritance if Mark died without children. Tristan offered to do all he could to find a wife for the king. Mark was unwilling to accede to his barons' requests, and he attempted to evade a decision by means of the following stratagem: one day a swallow let a long fair hair fall from its beak in front of Mark, and the king promptly declared that he would only marry the woman to whom that hair belonged. The barons were angry at this trick, but Tristan at once undertook to set out with a few chosen companions on the strange quest for this woman.

They set sail and it was not long before a storm blew them to the coast of Ireland, where they passed themselves off as merchants. Soon after their arrival they learned that the country was being laid waste by a dragon, which was doing so much harm that the Irish king had offered his daughter as a prize to the man who killed it. Unknown to his companions, Tristan set out to find the dragon and, after a fierce struggle, succeeded in killing it. He cut out its tongue and put it in his stocking; but the warmth made the poison in the tongue infuse Tristan's body and he fell to the ground, senseless. As he lay there, the Irish king's seneschal passed by and saw only the dead dragon. He hastily cut off its head and bore it triumphantly back to the palace, where he announced that he had slain the dragon. He thought that the dragon's real slayer must have been killed, and he claimed Yseut as his prize. The Irish king was surprised at the unexpected prowess of his cowardly seneschal and imposed a delay of a few days. Yseut was distressed at the thought of marrying the seneschal and certain that he could not have killed the dragon. With her mother and two maidservants she went to where the dragon's body lay, in the hope of finding its real slayer. They found Tristan, still unconscious, and without recognizing him took him back to the palace and tended his wounds. When he recovered his senses, Tristan told them he was the same Tantris they had looked after previously.

One day when Tristan was in the bath Yseut began to clean his sword. She noticed the notch in the blade, and compared it with the splinter taken from Morholt's skull. To her horror the piece fitted perfectly. She advanced angrily on Tristan, brandishing the sword and accusing him of being the slayer of her uncle. Tristan admitted this, but spoke quickly to calm Yseut. He said that he had killed

Morholt in fair combat, and pointed out that if she killed him she would have to marry the seneschal since only he could prove the seneschal's claim to be false. He finally calmed Yseut by telling her about the fair hair brought to King Mark by a swallow and of the quest he was engaged on. Yseut let Tristan live, and told her father that she had found the man who had really slain the dragon and that he would expose the seneschal's lie. At an assembly held next day the seneschal attempted to uphold his claim, but was confuted when Tristan produced the dragon's tongue. The Irish king learned Tristan's identity and pardoned him. Yseut was given to Tristan as a reward, and he announced that he would take her to Cornwall to become the wife of King Mark.

THE LOVE POTION

Before they left Ireland, Yseut's mother prepared a love potion which she entrusted to Brangain, Yseut's maid, and instructed her to give it to Yseut and her husband to drink on their wedding night.

Tristan and Yseut took leave of the Irish court and set out on the voyage to Cornwall. The third day was very hot and the ship was becalmed. While Tristan and Yseut were playing chess he called for a drink. By mistake, Brangain brought the love potion and handed it to Tristan, who drank and passed it to Yseut. Both thought it was good wine: neither knew that it held for them a lifetime of suffering and hardship and that it was to cause their destruction and their death. After some hesitation Tristan and Yseut confessed their love, and it was soon consummated.

As the ship neared Cornwall, Tristan and Yseut began to fear that Mark would discover what had happened. Accordingly they begged Brangain to take Yseut's place in Mark's bed on the wedding night. The unfortunate girl was at first reluctant, but finally acquiesced. When the ship arrived at the port of Tintagel, Tristan and Yseut were warmly welcomed by Mark and his people. The king was much struck with Yseut's beauty. The marriage of Mark and Yseut was celebrated soon after amid scenes of great festivity. When it was time for Mark and Yseut to retire Tristan conducted them to their chamber and extinguished all the lights, explaining that this was an Irish custom. Brangain took Yseut's place in bed without Mark noticing the substitution; when the king was asleep Yseut replaced Brangain and the deception was successfully accomplished. As time went on Mark showed Yseut great tenderness. Tristan and Yseut were able to meet in secret, and no one suspected their love.

THE ATTEMPTED MURDER
OF BRANGAIN

Yseut realized that Brangain constituted a potential danger, since she alone could betray the lovers to Mark. For her own safety, Yseut decided to have Brangain killed by two of her servants. One day they accompanied Brangain into the forest and suddenly drew their swords and seized her. Before killing her, they asked what wrong she had done to Yseut. She answered that her only misdeed was to lend Yseut a clean white tunic when Yseut's was soiled. The two men felt pity for her and, instead of killing her, bound her to a tree. They returned to Yseut and related what Brangain had told them. Yseut was deeply touched by Brangain's loyalty and at once ordered the men to bring her back. When Brangain appeared Yseut was overcome with remorse and begged her forgiveness. A reconciliation took place.

THE HARP AND THE ROTE

One day a strange knight came to Mark's court while Tristan was hunting in the forest. He played the rote before the king and Mark was so enchanted with his playing that he offered the knight any gift he chose. The knight chose Yseut and, since none of the Cornish barons dared fight in her defence, carried her off. As soon as Tristan learned of this he set out in pursuit and came up with the knight and Yseut at the water's edge. Tristan began to play his harp and greatly pleased the knight, who asked Tristan to accompany him and to take Yseut on horseback out to the waiting vessel. Once Yseut was on Tristan's horse they galloped back to court, where Tristan warned Mark to take better care of Yseut.

2

THE TRYST UNDER THE TREE

As Tristan and Yseut continued their illicit love they managed to deceive Mark but not the others at court. A group of barons hostile to Tristan, succeeded in arousing the king's suspicions concerning the relationship between his wife and his nephew. Mark forbade Tristan to remain at court for a time, and his nephew took lodgings in the town. With the help of Brangain, however, Tristan contrived to go on seeing Yseut. In the orchard surrounding the castle at Tintagel there was a stream; Tristan used to climb into the orchard at night and stand near the spring from which the stream flowed. He used to cut twigs and throw them into the stream which carried them to where Yseut could see them. As soon as she saw them she would hasten to join her lover in the orchard. But their meetings were discovered: at the instigation of Tristan's enemies a wicked dwarf, Frocin, found out by magic the secret of the lovers' rendezvous. Mark was told and his suspicions immediately increased. The dwarf swore that he could demonstrate the lovers' guilt and, acting on the dwarf's advice, Mark climbed one night into the branches of a tree near the spring, meaning to eavesdrop on their conversation.

When Tristan came to the spring he was able, in the moonlight, to see a reflection of the king's shadow. Yseut came into the orchard and also saw the king's shadow, much to her surprise; but she took care

that she gave no sign of

this. As she drew near to her lover, hear how she fore-
stalled him:

'Tristan, for God's sake, it is very wrong of you to
send for me at such a time!' Then she pretended to
weep. ['If the king were ever to hear of this meeting, I
am sure he would kill me.] For the sake of the Lord who
created all things, never send for me again. I am sorry to
say this, Tristan, but I am sure I should not dare to come.
The king thinks that I have been wicked enough to love
you. But before God I swear I have been loyal: may He
scourge me if anyone has ever had my love except the
man who had me as a maiden. There are villains in this
kingdom – and it was for their sake that you once fought
and killed Morholt – who are making the king believe, so
it seems to me, that you and I love each other. But you
have no desire for this; nor have I, by Almighty God,
any mind for a love which turns to sin. I would rather be
burned and have my ashes scattered to the winds any day
of my life than love someone who was not my rightful
lord. But, my God, he will not believe me! How little he
thinks of me now. Solomon was right when he said a
thief never likes the man who rescues him from the
gallows. If the villains in this land [remembered how
much they owe you, they would not talk of their sus-
picions about us, they would conceal them]. You had to
endure great pain from the wound my uncle gave you in
battle. I cured you: no wonder if you loved me for this!
And they have told the king you love me wickedly. Let
them go to heaven and God would turn his back on
them! Tristan, take care never to send for me anywhere
for anything; I should not dare to come. I have already

stayed here too long, without a word of a lie. If the king ever knew of this he would have me torn to pieces; it would be a horrible mistake, but I know he would kill me. Tristan, I am sure the king does not realize that I have loved you for his sake; I loved you because we were related. I used to think that my mother dearly loved my father's family, and she said that a wife who does not do so does not love her lord: I am certain this was right. I have loved you because of him and by doing this I have lost all his good will.'

['Certainly, he has shown that he suspects us.] His men have made him believe their lies about us.'

'Tristan, what do you mean? My lord the king is an honourable man: the idea that you and I have had wicked thoughts never came from him. But men can be led astray and made to forget good and do evil. This is what has happened to my lord. Tristan, I am going, I have stayed too long.'

'For God's sake, my lady! I asked you to come, and now that you are here I beg you to listen to what I have to say. I have always held you so dear.'

When he had heard his beloved speaking he knew that she had seen Mark. He thanked God for this, now that he was sure everything would go well.

'Ah, Yseut, you are a noble, honourable and loyal daughter of a king! Several times I have asked to see you since your room was forbidden to me and I could not speak to you. My lady, I want to beg your mercy on this poor wretch living in sorrow and hardship. That the king should ever think ill of me on your account grieves me so much that I think I shall die. It is hard for me [to bear these thoughts. He is doing me a great injustice. Alas, if only he knew my mind, he would know the truth straight away and] he would not believe these slanderers and send me away. The wicked, sly Cornishmen are very pleased with this and they are laughing over it. It looks to me now as though they wanted Mark to have no one of his own lineage around him. His marriage has done me much harm. God, why is the king so foolish? I would let him hang me before I became your lover. He will not even let me clear myself. He is angry with me because of his evil counsellors; he is very wrong to believe them, he does not realize how they have deceived him. I can remember one occasion when they kept very quiet: it was when Morholt came here, and not a single one of them dared take up his arms. My uncle was very much afraid then and would rather have been dead than alive. For the honour of the king I armed myself; I did battle with Morholt and drove him away. My dear uncle ought not to believe the slanders that are told about me; it makes me deeply angry to think of it. Does he not think he is wronging me? For he certainly is, by God! My lady, go straight to the king and tell him to have a fire made: I will walk into it, and if a single thread of my tunic is burnt then he can burn the rest of me; for I know there is no one at his court who would do battle with me. My lady, does your great kindness not move you to pity? Speak well of me to my uncle. I came to him from over the seas, and I want to return honourably.'

'Indeed, you are making a great mistake in asking me to tell him the truth and beg him to forgive you. I do not want to die yet nor ruin myself utterly! He thinks

ill of you on my account: am I to talk to him about this?
I should be very rash. I will not do it, Tristan, nor should
you ask me to. I am quite alone in this land. On my
account he has forbidden you to enter his chamber. It
would be madness for me to talk about it and I shall not
say a word. But I will tell you something I want you to
know: if he could forget his anger and his ill will and
pardon you, I should be very happy. But if he knew of
this meeting I know it would be death for us. I am going.
But I shall not be able to sleep. I am very much afraid
that someone may have seen us coming here. If the king
heard a word of our being together, I should not be
surprised if he decided to have me burnt. My body is
trembling with fear. I must go, I have been here far too
long.'

Yseut turned to go, but Tristan called her back.

'My lady, out of pity for his people, God took human
form and was born of a virgin; out of pity for me, please
advise me. I know you dare not remain here; but there is
no one I can talk to except you, for I know the king hates
me. All my weapons are pledged to him: let him give
them back to me and I will take my leave, for I dare not
stay. I know I am brave enough [for my service to be
welcome] in any land I go to. I know there is no court
in the world whose lord would not have me if I went
there. I have been glad to serve the king, Yseut, and by
my own head I tell you that before a year has passed he
will wish for all the gold in the world that he had not
thought of banishing me; and that is true. For God's
sake, Yseut, think of me, discharge me from the debt I
owe my host.'

'By God, Tristan, I marvel that you can ask me to do this! You are trying to do me harm, your request is not fair to me. You know what suspicion is, whether or not it is well-founded. By the glorious God who made heaven and earth and us, if the king were to hear a word of your wanting to be released from your pledges, he would obviously think you were disloyal. I could certainly not take this risk. You must realize that I am truly not saying this out of selfishness.'

Then Yseut went away and Tristan bade her farewell, weeping. Tristan leaned on a block of grey marble (to support himself, I think) and poured out his grief alone:

'God, fair St Evrol, I never thought to suffer such misfortune nor to leave in such poverty! I shall take neither weapons nor horse with me, nor any companion except Governal. God, nobody loves a man when he is out of favour! When I am in another land and I hear knights talking of war, I shall not dare to say a word. Now I have to suffer the hardships of fortune, which has caused me so much harm and brought me so much spite. My dear uncle, a man who mistrusts me with your wife does not know me; I never had any desire for such folly. [Whoever suspects me of such designs] knows very little of my heart.'

The king, who was up in the tree, had seen their meeting clearly and heard all that they said. The pity which filled him was so great that he could not for all the world hold back his tears; he was grief-stricken, and he began to hate the dwarf of Tintagel.

'Alas,' said the king, 'now I have seen that the dwarf deceived me greatly in persuading me to climb into this tree. He could not have shamed me more. He told me lies about my nephew, and for that I shall hang him. He made me so angry that I hated my wife. I acted like a fool when I believed him. He shall have his deserts: I will deal with him more harshly than Constantine did with Segestes, whom he had castrated when he found him with his wife. She had been crowned in Rome and many knights were in her service. She was dear to him and he honoured her; then he treated her badly and regretted it bitterly afterwards.'

Tristan had left a little while before. The king climbed down from the tree, thinking in his heart that now he would believe his wife and not the barons, who were trying to make him believe things which he knew were untrue and which he had proved to be false. Now he would not rest until he had given the dwarf such a reward that he would utter no more treason; nor would he ever again suspect Tristan and Yseut, but allow them to use his chamber freely as they wished.

'Now at last I know for certain. If what the dwarf told me had been true, their meeting would not have finished like this. If they loved each other wickedly, they had enough leisure here and I should have seen them kissing. But I heard them lamenting so much. I know now that they have no mind for it. Why did I believe such an outrageous accusation? That grieves me, and I repent of it; a man who believes everybody is a fool. I should have tried to find out the truth about these two before I had these wild suspicions. This has been a lucky evening for them! I have learned so much from their conversation that I shall never again be anxious about them. In the morning peace shall be made between Tristan and me, and he will have leave to be in my chamber at his pleasure. Now he will not depart in the morning as he intended.'

Hear now of the hunch-backed dwarf, Frocin. He was outside looking at the heavens, and he could see Orion and Venus. He knew the courses of the stars and he observed the planets. He knew what was to happen in the future: when he heard that a child was born, he could predict all the events of its life. The cunning dwarf had made every effort to deceive the man who was later to separate his soul from his body. He looked at the conjunction of the stars and his face flushed and swelled with rage, for he learned that the king was menacing him and would not rest until he had killed him. The dwarf soon lost his colour and went white; very quickly he took flight towards Wales. The king searched for the dwarf and was sorry that he could not be found.

Yseut went to her room. Brangain could see that she was pale and knew she had heard something that had upset her, for her colour had changed and her face was white. [Brangain asked her what was the matter] and Yseut replied:

'Fair maid, I have good reason to be sad and anxious. Brangain, I will tell you everything. I do not know who wanted to betray us today, but King Mark was in the tree by the marble block; I saw his shadow in the spring. God let me speak first. Not a word was said of what I had gone there for, I assure you, but there was a great deal of lamenting and complaining. I reproached him for sending for me, and he in turn begged me to reconcile him to my lord, who was greatly mistaken about him on my account. And I told him he was very foolish to ask me and said I would never come again, nor would I talk to the king about it. I do not know what more I said – there was a lot of complaining! The king did not notice anything, nor did he see through what I said. I got myself out of a difficult situation.'

Brangain was very glad to hear this: 'Yseut, my lady, God is always true. He has been very kind to us when he let you finish your conversation without doing anything else, so that the king saw nothing that cannot be easily explained. God has really worked a miracle for you. He is a true father, and he will not harm those who are loyal and good.'

Tristan also told Governal how he had behaved. Governal listened, and thanked God that Tristan had done no more with his beloved.

The king failed to find his dwarf (God, so much the worse for Tristan!). Mark then went to his room. Yseut was very frightened when she saw him.

'Sire, for God's sake, where have you come from? Why do you come alone?'

'My queen, I have come to speak to you and to ask you something. Do not conceal anything from me, I want to know the truth.'

'Sire, I have never lied to you. Even if I am to die now I shall tell you the whole truth, not a single word shall be false.'

'My lady, have you seen my nephew?'

'Sire, I will tell you the whole truth. You will not believe it, but I shall speak without deceit. I have seen your nephew and spoken to him; I met him under the pine tree. Now kill me for this, king, if you want to. Certainly I saw him. It is a great sorrow to me that you should think I love Tristan shamefully and deceitfully. I am so upset that I do not care if you make me come to a wretched end. My Lord, have pity on me now! I have told you the truth. Yet you will not believe me, instead you believe vain and foolish words. May my good faith acquit me! Tristan, your nephew, went to the pine tree over there in the garden and sent to ask me to go to him. He had nothing to say, but I could not show him too little respect since it is through him that I am your queen. Certainly, if it were not for those wretches who tell you of things that never were, I should willingly pay him honour. You are my lord, sire, and everyone knows he is your nephew; because of you I have loved him much, sire. But the wicked slanderers, who want to have him sent away from court, are making you believe lies. Now Tristan is going. May God make them ashamed of this! I spoke with your nephew last night; he lamented greatly because of his sorrow and asked me to reconcile him with you. I told him to go away and never to send for me again, for I should not come to him; nor would I ever speak to you about it. Sire, you will not believe any of this! That was all. Kill me if you want to, but it will be wrong. Because of this strife Tristan is leaving and I know he will cross the sea. He asked me to pay for his lodging. I did not want to pay anything on his behalf nor even speak to him for long. Sire, now I have told you the truth without fail. If I lie to you, cut off my head. You may be sure, sire, that I would gladly pay his debts if I dared; but I even hesitated to put four small coins in his purse on account of your gossiping household. He is going away poor, may God guide him! You are driving him out through a great error. He will never come back to this land if God is his true friend.'

The king well knew that she was speaking the truth, for he had heard all those words. He embraced her and kissed her a hundred times. She wept and he told her to be quiet: never again at any time would he mistrust them because of what any slanderer said; they could come and go as they wished; Tristan's goods were his and his were Tristan's; never would he believe those Cornishmen again. Then the king told the queen how the wicked dwarf Frocin had warned him of their meeting and made him climb into the tree that evening to watch them.

'Were you in the pine tree, then, sire?'

'Yes, my lady, by St Martin! Nothing was said, however slight, that I did not hear. When I heard Tristan recall the battle which I made him fight, I felt such pity that I all but fell from the tree. I was overcome with grief when I heard you recount his suffering at sea from the wound the dragon gave him,[1] which you cured and you were very good to him; when he asked you to redeem his pledges, you did not want to acquit him. Nor did either of you try to approach the other. Up in the tree I felt such sympathy for you, I could only smile to myself.'

'My Lord, I am very glad of this. Now you know with certainty, for that would have been a fine opportunity

1. See Notes, pp. 166–7.

for us. If he loved me wickedly, you would have seen signs enough. On the contrary, by my faith, you saw that there was no hint of his coming up to kiss me or behave in an unseemly way. Surely, Tristan's love for me is blameless. Sire, if you had not seen us just now you would certainly not have believed me.'

'I would not, by God,' said the king. 'Brangain, God give you honour, go and find my nephew in his lodging. If he says one thing and another and will not come for you, say that it is I who am sending for him.'

'Sire,' said Brangain, 'he hates me. God knows he is wrong, but he says that it is through me that he has quarrelled with you and he is eager to get rid of me. But I will go, for your sake he will refrain from touching me. Sire, reconcile me with him when he comes here.' (Just listen to the deceitful woman! She spoke like a real swindler. She lied deliberately and complained about Tristan's ill will.) 'I am going for him, sire,' said Brangain, 'you will do me a good turn if you can restore me to his favour.'

The king replied: 'I will try hard. Go quickly, then, and bring him here.'

Yseut was pleased at this, and the king even more so. Brangain ran out of the door. Tristan was standing by the wall, where he had heard them talking to the king. He caught Brangain in his arms and embraced her, thanking God [that the king was going to allow him] to be with Yseut as he wished. Brangain said to Tristan:

'Sir, there in his chamber the king has been deliberating about you and your dear love. He is no longer angry with you, and now he hates those who are trying to trap you. He has asked me to come to you. I told him you were angry with me. Make a show of being asked and not coming easily. If the king asks you for something on my behalf, pretend to look angry.'

Tristan embraced her and kissed her, he was so happy and relieved. They went to the curtained room where the king and Yseut were, and Tristan entered.

'Nephew,' said the king, 'come forward. Forgive Brangain for what has made you angry, and I will forgive you.'

'Uncle, my dear lord, listen to me. That is a very slight apology to make after you have deeply wounded me by making grave accusations of such great wrong-doing and wickedness. If they had been true I should have been damned, and Yseut would have been dishonoured. God knows we never thought of it. You know now that the man who makes you believe such incredible things hates you. From now on take better advice and do not bear malice against the queen or against me, for I am of your own blood.'

'I shall not do so, fair nephew, by my faith.'

So Tristan and the king were reconciled. The king gave him leave to go into his chamber – how happy he was! Tristan came and went to the chamber and the king took no notice.

3

THE FLOUR ON THE FLOOR

WHO can be in love for a year or two and not reveal it? For love cannot be concealed. Often one lover would wink at the other, often they would speak together both alone and in the sight of others. They could not find their pleasure everywhere and they had to meet many times.

At Mark's court there were three barons – you never saw more wicked men! They had sworn that, if King Mark did not make his nephew leave the country, they would tolerate it no longer and would retire to their castles to make war on the king. For one day, under a tree in the garden, they had seen Yseut the Fair with Tristan in a place that no man should allow. And they had often seen them lying together, naked, in Mark's bed. When the king went into the forest, Tristan would say: 'Sire, I am coming,' and stay back and go into the king's chamber and remain there for a long time with Yseut.

'We ourselves must tell the king. Let us go to the king and say, whether he loves us or hates us, that we want his nephew driven away.'

They came to this decision together. Then they took King Mark to one side and said: 'Sire, things are going badly. Your nephew and Yseut love each other, and anyone who wants to can find out. We will not tolerate this any longer.'

The king heard this, sighed and bent his head. He walked up and down, not knowing what to say.

'King,' said the three villains, 'we will not consent to this any longer, for we know it is true that you are conniving at their wickedness. You know all about this extraordinary thing. What are you going to do about it? Now be advised! If you do not banish your nephew from court so that he never returns, we shall no longer support you nor keep peace with you. We shall make our neighbours leave the court, for we cannot put up with this. We can set out the problem for you quickly; now tell us your wishes.'

'My lords, you are loyal to me. As God is my help, I marvel that my nephew should have sought my shame; but he has served me in a strange way. Give me your advice, I beg you. You must advise me well, for I do not want to lose your service. You know I have no wish to act arrogantly.'

'Sire, then send for the prophetic dwarf. There is no doubt that he is very clever, and a plan will soon be made. Send for the dwarf, then everything will be settled.'

And he came very quickly (cursed be the hunchback!). One of the barons embraced him, and the king revealed why they had sent for him. Now hear what treachery and corruption this dwarf Frocin proposed to the king. (Cursed be all such magicians! Whoever would have thought of such wickedness as this dwarf did? May God curse him!)

'Tell your nephew that he must go in the morning to King Arthur in walled Carlisle. He is to take to Arthur as fast as he can a letter written on parchment, well sealed and fastened with wax. King, Tristan sleeps at the foot of your bed. Soon, during the night, I know that he will want to talk to Yseut and, by God, he will have to go to her. King, leave the room in the early part of the night. I swear to you by God and the Law of Rome, if Tristan loves her wickedly he will go to see her. If he does go, and I do not know and you do not see him, then kill me and all your men. Otherwise, their guilt will be proved without any trial. King, leave me now to my work and let me try to predict what will happen. Do not tell him of the message until it is time for bed.'

The king replied: 'It shall be done, my friend.'

Then they separated, each going his own way. The dwarf was extremely cunning, and he did a very underhand thing. He went to a baker and bought four pennyworth of flour and tied the bags to his tunic. (Whoever would think of such a low trick?) That night, when the king had eaten, they lay down to sleep in the hall. Tristan led the king to his bed.

'Fair nephew,' said the king, 'I have a task for you; see that you carry out my wishes. You must ride as far as Carlisle to King Arthur and give him this letter to open. Nephew, give him greetings from me and do not stay there more than a day.'

Tristan heard what he was to do, and replied that he would carry the letter: 'King, I shall set out in the morning.'

'Yes, before daybreak.'

Tristan was very agitated. Between his bed and the king's there was fully the length of a lance. Tristan had a wild idea: he said to himself that he would talk to the

queen, if he could, after his uncle had gone to sleep.
(God, what folly! He was too rash.). The dwarf slept in
the same room. Hear what he did that night: he spread
the flour between the two beds so that the footsteps
would appear if one went to the other during the night,
for flour holds the shape of footprints. Tristan saw the
dwarf busy scattering the flour. He wondered what this
could mean, since he did not usually do so. Then he
realized:

'Soon this place will be covered with flour to show
our footprints if one of us goes to the other. It would be
folly to go to her now that he will be able to see.'

The day before in the forest Tristan had been wounded
in the leg by a large boar, and this hurt him greatly. The
wound had bled very much and it was not bound up, to
his misfortune. Tristan did not go to sleep, I believe.
At midnight the king arose and went out of the room.
With him went the hunch-backed dwarf. It was dark
inside the room, no lamp or candle was lit. Tristan rose
to his feet. (God, why did he do this? Now listen!) He
put his feet together, judged the distance, leaped and
landed on the king's bed. His wound opened and bled a
great deal; the blood which came out soaked the sheets.
The wound was bleeding but he did not feel it, for he
was too intent on his pleasure. The blood gathered in
several places. The dwarf was outside; by the moonlight
he could see that the two lovers were lying together. He
trembled with joy and said to the king:

'If you cannot take them together, go and hang me!'

The three villains who secretly planned this treachery
were also there. The king came in. Tristan heard him

coming, rose from the bed in alarm and hastily leaped back to his own. In the leap which Tristan made the blood fell (what bad luck!) from his wound on to the flour. (God, what a pity the queen did not take the sheets off the bed! Neither of them would have been caught that night. If she had thought of it, she could easily have protected her honour. God worked a miracle here when it pleased Him to safeguard them.) The king came back into the room; the dwarf was with him, holding a candle. Tristan was pretending to be asleep and snoring loudly. He was alone in the room except for Perinis, who lay at his feet without stirring, and the queen lying in her bed. On the flour the warm blood could be seen. The king noticed the blood in the bed, the white sheets were red with it. And on the flour there were traces of the leap. The king threatened Tristan. The three barons came into the room, angrily they took Tristan in his bed. Because of his prowess they had begun to hate him, and also the queen. They abused her and threatened her. They would not rest until justice was done. They could see Tristan's leg bleeding.

'This is only too clear proof. You are guilty,' said the king, 'you will only waste your time trying to defend yourself. Tristan, you may be sure that you will be put to death tomorrow.'

'Mercy, sire,' he cried, 'for the sake of Our Lord who suffered His passion, have pity on us, sire!'

But the villains said: 'Sire, avenge yourself!'

'Fair uncle, it does not matter about me. I know I have come to my end. Had it not been for angering you, though, the barons would have paid dearly for this.

Never, by their eyes, would they have thought of laying their hands on me but for your presence. But I have no quarrel with you. Now do what you will with me, for good or ill, and I am ready to suffer it. But, sire, for God's sake, have pity on the queen.' Tristan bowed his head. 'There is no man in your household, if he uttered the treason that I have wrongly and wickedly loved the queen, who would not find me armed in the field. Sire, mercy on her, for God's sake!'

The three barons who were in the room had taken Tristan prisoner and bound him. Then they bound the queen, and Tristan became very angry. If he had known that he was not going to be allowed to defend himself, he would have risked being torn to pieces rather than let himself and Yseut be captured. But so great was his trust in God that he firmly believed that, if he were allowed to defend himself, nobody would dare to take up arms against him. He counted on being able to defend himself in combat. For this reason he did not want his behaviour to Mark to be incorrect through any hasty action. But if he had known how things were and what was to happen to them, he would have killed all three barons and the king could not have protected them. (God, why did he not kill them? He would have been in a much better position.)

4

THE CONDEMNATION AND ESCAPE
OF THE LOVERS

THE cry went through the city that Tristan and Queen Yseut had been found together and that the king wanted to put them to death. Old and young wept, and said to each other:

'Alas, we have much to weep for! Alas, Tristan, noble knight! What a shame that these wretches have had you taken by treachery. Noble, honoured queen, in what land will a king's daughter be born who is your equal? Dwarf, your magic has done this! If anyone finds the dwarf anywhere and does not pass his sword through his body, may he never see the face of God! Alas, Tristan, there will be such grief for you, fair sweet friend, brought to such distress! Alas, what sadness your death will cause! When Morholt came to the port here to take away our children our barons quickly fell silent, for none of them was brave enough to take up arms against him. You undertook the battle for all of us in Cornwall and killed Morholt. He gave you a wound with his spear which nearly killed you. We should never let you be put to death.'

The noise and the tumult rose. Everyone ran straight to the palace. The king was very harsh and angry; none of the barons was strong enough or bold enough to dare to speak to the king and ask him to pardon this misdeed. The night ended and at daybreak the king ordered thorns to be brought and a ditch made in the ground. Holding a knife in his hand, the king sent everywhere for vines to put with the white and black thorns and roots. It was already the first hour of the day. It was proclaimed throughout the kingdom that everyone should come to court. They came as quickly as they could until all the Cornish people were assembled. In all the noise and commotion there was no one who did not lament, excepting only the dwarf of Tintagel. The king addressed them, saying that he was going to burn his wife and his nephew on a pyre. All the people of the kingdom cried out:

'King, you would do them too great a wrong if they were not first brought to trial. Afterwards put them to death. Sire, mercy!'

The king replied angrily: 'By the Lord who created the world and all things in it, not even if I were to lose my inheritance would I hold back from burning them. If anyone ever thinks of speaking to me about this, I warn you now to leave me completely in peace.'

He ordered them to light the fire and bring his nephew out. He wanted to burn him first. They went to fetch him and the king waited. Then they dragged Tristan out (by God, they acted badly!). He wept much but it was of no avail for they led him on shamefully. Yseut wept and nearly went out of her mind.

'Tristan,' she cried, 'what grief that you are so shamefully bound! Even if I were killed it would be a great joy to me if you escaped, fair friend. Vengeance would yet be taken.'

Hear now, my lords, of the Lord God, of how He is

full of pity; He does not seek the death of a sinner. He had heard the cries and laments of the poor people for those who were going to their death. On the way they would pass a chapel on a hill, built on a ledge of rock. It overlooked the sea, facing north. That part which is called the chancel was raised; beyond it was only the cliff. The slope there was all slate; if a squirrel leaped over he would be dead, for he could not come down safely. In the apse was a window of red glass which a holy man had placed there.

Tristan called to his captors: 'Lords, here is a chapel. For God's sake, let me go in. My time is nearly at an end. I shall pray God to have mercy on me, for I have sinned greatly against Him. Lords, there is only this way in, and each of you is carrying a sword. You know that I cannot get out, I shall have to return to you. When I have ended my prayer I shall return to you as I say.'

Then they said to each other: 'We can let him go in.' They loosed his bonds and he went in. Tristan did not move slowly. He went to the window behind the altar, pulled it towards him with his right hand and leaped through the opening. He would rather jump than be burnt before that assembly. My lords, there was a big, wide stone in the middle of those rocks; Tristan jumped on to it very easily. The wind caught his clothes and prevented him from crashing to the ground – Cornishmen still call this stone 'Tristan's Leap'. The chapel was full of people. Tristan jumped to his feet, the sand was soft. They were all on their knees in the church. The others were waiting outside the church, but in vain. Tristan was fleeing, God had shown him great mercy. He ran along the beach with great strides, and he could hear the fire crackling. He had no mind to return and ran as fast as he could.

But now hear of Governal. With his sword at his side he had gone out of the city on horseback. He knew that if he was overtaken the king would have him burnt on account of his master. Fear made him take flight. Tristan's companion held him very dear and he had not wanted to leave Tristan's sword behind. He had taken it down and was carrying it with his own. Tristan caught sight of his companion, recognized him at once and hailed him. Governal came up joyfully.

'Master, God has had great mercy on me. I have escaped and here I am. Alas, what does this matter to me? If I have not got Yseut, the leap I made just now is worth nothing to me. Why did I not simply kill myself? It may bring me much grief that I have escaped. Yseut, you are to be burnt. I escaped in vain. She is being burnt for me, I shall die for her!'

Governal said: 'For God's sake, fair sir, be consoled and do not despair. Here is a thick bush surrounded by a ditch. Let us get inside. Many people pass by here, you will hear news of Yseut. And if she is burnt, never get into the saddle again if you do not take vengeance immediately afterwards! You will not go unaided. By Jesus, the Son of Mary, I should never rest inside a house until the three wicked villains who had killed your love Yseut had met their deaths. If you were killed now, fair sir, before vengeance had been taken, I should never be happy again.'

69

Tristan replied: 'This vexes you greatly, I know. Fair master, I have not got my sword.'

'Yes, you have. I brought it with me.'

'Good, master,' said Tristan, 'now I fear nothing any more, save God.'

'I have under my tunic something else which will be useful to you and which you will be glad to see: a strong, light hauberk, which may well be of service to you.'

'In God's name,' said Tristan, 'give it to me. By that God I believe in, I would rather be torn to pieces – if I can reach the fire in time, before my love is thrown on it – than fail to kill the men who are holding her captive.'

Governal said: 'Do not be in a hurry. God may give you a far better chance to avenge yourself, when you will not have the trouble that you might have now. I cannot now see any of your men, for the king is furiously angry with you. All the citizens and the townsmen are in his allegiance. He gave them all, publicly, the command that if anyone can ever capture you and fails to do so he will be hanged. Every man loves himself more than he loves you. If a hue and cry was raised for you, a man might well want to let you go free but he would not even dare to think of it.'

Tristan wept and was vexed. In spite of all the men of Tintagel, and even if he were to be torn to pieces, he would never have restrained himself from going straight to his love if his master had not forbidden him.

A messenger ran into Yseut's room and told her not to weep, for her lover had escaped.

'Thank God!' she said, 'now it does not matter if they kill me or keep me bound or set me loose.'

As the three barons had advised, the king had had her bound, and her wrists were tied so tightly that blood was being squeezed from all her fingers. 'By God,' she said, 'if ever [I lament my own fate now] that the wicked slanderers who had to guard my lover have lost him, thank God, then no one should ever think well of me again. I know that the mischief-making dwarf and the jealous villains who plotted my death will get their deserts. May it be their ruin!'

My lords, news came to the king that his nephew had escaped through the chapel while he was being taken to be burnt. Mark's face darkened with rage, he could scarcely contain himself for wrath. Angrily he sent for Yseut. She came out of the hall and there was tumult in the streets. When they saw how the lady was bound – it was shameful – they were very shocked. Who would believe what grief they showed for her, how they cried to God for pity:

'Noble, honoured queen, what sorrow those who stirred up this affair have brought to the country! They will surely be able to put their gains in a very small purse. May great harm come to them for this!'

The queen was led towards the fire, where the thorns were burning. Dinas, the lord of Dinan, who loved Tristan greatly, fell at the king's feet.

'Sire,' he said, 'listen to me. I have served you truly and loyally for a long time. There is not a man in all this kingdom, not even a poor orphan or an old woman, who would give me a penny for the position of seneschal which I have held at your court all my life. Sire, mercy on the queen! You want to burn her without trial, but this is not rightful for the crime has not been proved. It will be a great shame if you burn her. Sire, Tristan has escaped. He knows the country well, the plains, the fields, the passes and the fords, and he is fierce. You are his uncle and he is your nephew: he would do you no harm. But if your barons fell into his power, would he not ill-treat them? Your land would be laid waste. For myself, sire, I would not deny that if even a squire was burnt or killed for my sake by anyone, if he were king over seven lands he would give them all to me as compensation before I was amply revenged. Do you think it would not cause Tristan the deepest grief to see the death of such a noble lady, whom he brought here from a distant kingdom? There would be great strife over this. King, give her to me as a reward for serving you all my life.'

The three who had caused all this had become deaf and dumb. They knew that Tristan had escaped and were in great fear that he might ambush them. The king took Dinas' hand and swore angrily by St Thomas that he would not rest until justice had been done and she had been put on the fire. Dinas heard him and was very sad, it grieved him deeply. By his wish the queen would never have been put to death. He rose to his feet and kept his head bowed.

'King, I am going to Dinan. By the Lord who made Adam, I would not see her burnt for all the gold and all the possessions that belonged to the richest men that have lived since the days when Rome was glorious.'

He mounted his charger and rode away with bowed head, vexed and sorrowing. Yseut was led to the fire. She was surrounded by people all crying and shouting and cursing the king's traitors. Tears ran down her cheeks. The lady was clad in a tight tunic of dark grey silk, laced with a fine gold thread. Her hair fell to her feet, she had tressed it with gold thread. Whoever had seen her body and her face would have had an evil heart if he had not taken pity on her. Her arms were bound very tightly.

There was a leper in Lantyan, his name was Ivain and he was terribly infirm. He had hurried up to see what was going on. He had a good hundred companions with him, carrying their sticks and crutches. You never saw people so ugly or hunched or deformed. Each was holding his clapper. Ivain called hoarsely to the king:

'Sire, you wish to do justice by burning your wife like this. It is a harsh punishment but, if ever I knew anything, it will not last long. That great fire will soon burn her and the wind will scatter her ashes. The fire will subside and all that is left of her punishment will be cinders. That is the punishment you are going to give her. But, if you would listen to me [I could tell you of a way to punish her so] that she would rather have been put to death than be still living in dishonour. Anyone who came to hear of this would think the more of you. King, would you like to do this?'

The king listened and said: 'If you can tell me, without a trick, how she may live and be dishonoured, I shall be grateful to you. Take something of mine, if you wish. No manner of death is so grim and horrible that I shall not love for ever, by God the king, that man who today can choose the worst for her!'

Ivain answered: 'I can tell you quickly what I have in

mind. Look, here I have a hundred companions. Give Yseut to us and we will possess her in common. No woman ever had a worse end. Sire, there is such lust in us that no woman on earth could tolerate intercourse with us for a single day. The very clothes stick to our bodies. With you she used to be honoured and happily clad in blue and grey furs. She learned of good wines in your marble halls. If you give her to us lepers, when she sees our low hovels and looks at our dishes and has to sleep with us – in place of your fine meals, sire, she will have the pieces of food and crumbs that are left for us at the gates – then, by the Lord who dwells above, when she sees our court and all its discomforts she would rather be dead than alive. The snake Yseut will know then that she has been wicked! She would rather have been burnt.'

The king listened to him, stood up and said nothing for a long while. He had heard what Ivain had said. He ran to Yseut and took her by the hand. Yseut cried out:

'Sire, mercy! Burn me here instead of giving me to them!'

The king handed her over to the lepers, and a good hundred crowded around her. Everyone who heard the noise and the shouting took pity on her. But whoever might be sorrowful, Ivain was happy. He led Yseut away along the sandy path. The other lepers – not one who did not have a crutch – went in a throng straight towards where Tristan was waiting in ambush. Governal saw them and shouted:

'My son, what are you going to do? There is your love!'

'God,' said Tristan, 'what good fortune! Alas, lovely

Yseut, to think that you were to die for me and I for you!
Those people that have got their hands on you can all be
sure of this, that if they do not let you go straight away
I shall make some of them sorry.'

He struck his horse and sprang out of the bush,
shouting as loud as he could: 'Ivain, you have taken her
far enough. Let her go now or I will cut off your head
with this sword!'

Ivain began to take off his cloak and shouted to the
lepers: 'Now, crutches in your hands! Now we shall see
who is on our side.'

You should have seen those lepers panting as they took
off their coats and their cloaks! Each of them was shaking
his crutch, some threatening, others fighting. Tristan
did not want to touch them or strike them on the head
and wound them. Governal came out as the shout went
up, holding a stick of green oak in his hand. He struck
Ivain, who was holding Yseut, and the blood ran down
to his feet. Tristan helped his master and grasped
Yseut's right hand. (Some story-tellers say they drowned
Ivain, but they are fools and they do not know the story
at all well. Beroul has a better memory of it: Tristan was
too noble and too courtly to kill such people.) Tristan
went off with the queen. They left the plain and all three
went into the forest. Yseut rejoiced, she was suffering no
longer.

5

THE FOREST OF MORROIS

THEY slept that night in the forest of Morrois on a hillside. Tristan was as safe now as if he had been in a walled castle. Tristan was a skilled archer and could make good use of a bow. Governal had taken one from a forester it belonged to and had also carried off two arrows with the tips and feathers already fitted. Tristan took the bow and went into the wood. He saw a roe-deer, fitted an arrow to the string, shot, and the arrow sank deep into the right side of the deer. With a cry it leaped up and then fell to the ground. Tristan picked up the beast and took it back. Then he made a dwelling place. With his sword he cut branches to make a leafy bower and Yseut covered the ground thickly with leaves. Tristan sat down with the queen. Governal knew how to cook and made a good fire from some dry wood. (Cooks have a great deal to do!) They had no milk or salt in this lodging. The queen was worn out on account of all that she had gone through; she felt drowsy and wanted to go to sleep with her head resting on her lover. My lords, they stayed for a long time deep in the forest, living like this. They were long in that deserted countryside.

6

KING MARK'S HORSE'S EARS

HEAR now what the dwarf did to the king. The dwarf knew a secret of the king's, and only he knew it. Very wrongly he revealed it. He acted like a fool, for afterwards the king cut off his head. One day the dwarf was drunk and the barons asked him what it meant that he and the king were talking secretly together.

'He has always found me faithful,' said the dwarf, 'in keeping a secret of his well hidden. I can see that you want to hear it, but I do not wish to break my word to the king. I will lead the three of you to the Gué Aventuros. There is a hawthorn bush there with a ditch by its roots. I can push my head into it and you will hear me speaking outside. What I shall say will be the king's secret, which I am bound to keep.'

The barons went to the hawthorn with dwarf Frocin leading them. The dwarf was short with a big head. He soon reached the ditch and they pushed him in up to his shoulders.

'Now listen, lord marquises! I am talking to you, hawthorn bush, not to the barons. Mark has horse's ears!'

They heard quite clearly what the dwarf said. One day King Mark was talking to his barons after dinner, holding a bow of laburnum wood in his hand. The three to whom the dwarf had told the secret came up and said privately to the king:

'King, we know your secret.'

The king laughed and said: 'This affliction, that I have horse's ears, happened to me because of that magician. I am resolved to make an end of him.' He drew his sword and cut off the dwarf's head. Many people were glad of this, for they hated the dwarf Frocin because of what he had done to Tristan and the queen.

7

THE HERMIT OGRIN. I

MY lords, you have heard how Tristan had leaped over the cliff on to the rocks, and how Governal had fled on horseback because he feared burning if Mark captured him. Now they were together in the forest where Tristan fed them on venison. They were a long time in the wood. Each morning they had to leave the place where they had spent the night. One day they came by chance to the hermitage of Friar Ogrin. They were leading a rough and hard life, but they loved each other with such true love that neither felt any hardship because of the other. The hermit was leaning on his staff and recognized Tristan. Hear how he addressed him:

'Sir Tristan, a proclamation has been made on oath throughout Cornwall that whoever gives you up to the king will be sure to receive a hundred silver marks in reward. There is no baron in this land who has not pledged his hand to the king to deliver you to him dead or alive.' Ogrin went on in a kind voice: 'Truly, Tristan,

78

God will pardon the sin of a man who repents in good faith by making confession.'

Tristan said to him: 'Indeed, sir, you do not know the reason for her love for me. It is because of a love potion that she loves me. I cannot part from her nor she from me. That is the truth.'

Ogrin answered: 'And what consolation can be given to a man who is dead? For a man who lives in sin for a long time is dead if he does not repent. No one can give absolution to a sinner if he does not repent.'

The hermit Ogrin exhorted them and advised them to repent. He told them of the prophecies of Holy Writ, and often reminded them of their estrangement from the court. He said firmly to Tristan: 'What are you going to do? Now think!'

'Sir, I love Yseut so much. Because of her I cannot sleep nor even doze. My decision is soon taken: I would rather be a beggar with her and live on herbs and acorns than possess the kingdom of the rich King Otran. I beg you not to ask me to leave her, for I cannot do so.'

Yseut wept at the hermit's feet, now blushing and now going pale. She implored his pity:

'Sir, by Almighty God, he loves me and I love him only because of a draught that I drank and he drank. That was our misfortune. Because of this the king has driven us out.'

The hermit answered her: 'May God who created the world give you true repentance!'

They stayed that night with the hermit, who put himself to great trouble for their sake. In the morning Tristan and Yseut departed. They remained in the

wood and avoided the open country. They were troubled
at being short of bread. Tristan killed many stag, hind
and roe-deer in the wood. Where they made their abode
they could make a big fire to do their cooking, but they
could only spend one night in each place. My lords, hear
how the king had issued a proclamation concerning
Tristan – there was no parish in Cornwall where the
news did not cause dismay – saying that whoever found
Tristan should raise the cry.

8

TRISTAN'S DOG

ANYONE who would like to hear a story about the virtues
of a good upbringing, listen to me for a while! You will
hear me tell of a hunting dog so fine that no king or
count had a dog to equal him. He was fast, always on the
alert, quick and lively, and his name was Husdant. He
was in Mark's castle on a leash fastened to a block of
wood. He looked all round him and was very upset
because he could not see his master. He would not eat
bread or paste or anything that was given to him. He
scowled and pawed the ground with tears in his eyes.
Many people felt pity for the dog. Everyone said:

'If he were mine, I should let him off the leash. It
would be a shame if he were to go mad. There was never
a dog like Husdant, always so quick and now so sad for
his master. There was never such a loving animal.
Solomon spoke truly when he said that his dog was his

friend. Husdant, you are the proof of this. Since your master was captured you would not eat anything. King, let him off the leash!'

The king thought the dog was going mad because of his master and said to himself: 'This dog is certainly very intelligent. I do not think that in our time there has been a knight as valiant as Tristan in the land of Cornwall.'

The three Cornish barons addressed the king: 'Sire, set Husdant free. Then we shall know for certain whether he is miserable because of his master. If he is mad, he will no sooner be untied than he will bite someone, beast or man; he will be slavering at the jaws.'

The king called a squire to set Husdant free. All the onlookers climbed on seats or on their saddles for they were afraid of which way he might turn at first. They all said Husdant was mad. But the dog paid them no attention. As soon as he was set free he ran through the rows of people without hesitating. He went out through the door of the hall to the lodging place where he could usually find Tristan. The king and the others who were following saw this. The dog barked and growled and showed his grief. Then he picked up his master's scent. Tristan did not take a single step after he had been captured and was being led to the fire that the dog did not follow. Everyone urged him on. Husdant went into the room where Tristan was treacherously captured, then left it and ran, jumping and barking, to the chapel. People were still following the dog, but once he was let off the leash he did not stop until he reached the church built high on the cliff. The nimble, swift Husdant entered by the chapel door, jumped on to the altar, could not see his master, and left by the window. He scrambled down the cliff, scratching his leg, put his nose to the ground and barked. Husdant paused for a moment at the place where Tristan had waited in ambush at the flower-strewn edge of the wood. Then he went on and ran into the forest. No one saw him who did not take pity on him. The knights said to the king:

'Let us stop following the dog. He might lead us to somewhere it would be difficult to get back from.'

They gave up chasing the dog and turned back. Husdant came upon a cart-track and was glad to find a pathway. The whole wood rang with the sound of his barking. Tristan was deep in the wood with the queen and Governal. They heard the noise and Tristan listened intently.

'By my faith,' he said, 'I can hear Husdant.'

They were startled and alarmed. Tristan leaped up and drew his bow, and they retired into a thicket. It was King Mark they were afraid of, for they said in dismay that he would be coming with the dog. The dog knew the path and it was not long before he reached them. When he saw Tristan he recognized him as his master and shook himself vigorously, wagging his tail. Whoever had seen the dog was all wet with joy could have said that he never saw such joy! He ran up to Yseut the Fair and then to Governal. He greeted them all joyfully, even the horse. Tristan felt very sorry for the dog.

'God,' he said, 'what a pity this dog has followed us. A dog who does not keep quiet in the wood is no good to a man who has been banished. We are in the wood and the king hates us. He is hunting us, my lady, in the fields and in the forest. If he found us and captured us he would have us burned or hanged. We have no need of a dog. You may be certain of one thing: if Husdant stays with us we shall be afraid and anxious. Better for him to be killed than for us to be captured because of his barking. I regret very much that he will have to die, for he is a fine animal. It was his greatness of heart that led him here. But how can I get out of it? I certainly regret that I have to kill him. Help me, give me your advice. We must protect ourselves.'

Yseut said to him: 'Have pity on him, my lord! A dog barks when it is hunting, both by its nature and by habit. I heard a story once, soon after Arthur was made king, that a Welsh forester owned a hound which he had trained in a special way. If he wounded a stag with an arrow and it bled, the dog would bound after it whatever track it fled along and however close to its prey the dog was it never barked or made any noise. It would be a good thing if we could train Husdant not to bark when he was out hunting and pursuing his prey.'

Tristan stood listening. He was full of pity. He thought a little, then said: 'If I could train Husdant by my efforts to be silent instead of barking I should be very glad to have him. And I shall try to do this before the week is out. I should be very sorry to kill him, but I am greatly afraid of the dog's bark. For I might be somewhere with you and Governal, and if the dog barked he would have us captured. Now I will try to teach him to hunt game without barking.'

Then Tristan went into the wood to hunt. He made

ready and shot a deer, which started to bleed. The dog barked. The wounded deer leaped away, lively Husdant barked loudly and the wood resounded with the noise. Tristan struck the dog hard. Husdant came to a halt beside his master, stopped barking and gave up the chase. He looked up at his master, not knowing what to do. He dared not bark and he stopped following the deer. Tristan bent down to push the dog and cleared a way ahead with a stick. Husdant wanted to bark again. So Tristan began to teach him. Before a month had passed the dog was trained to follow his prey on the moor without barking. He never let a beast get away, on snow, grass or ice, however fast and nimble it was. The dog became a great help to them and did them a great deal of good. If he took a roe-buck or a deer in the wood he hid it well and covered it with branches. If he took his game on the open moor, and it happened that he took many there, he threw grass over it and returned to his master to lead him to where the beast was. Dogs are very useful creatures!

9

GOVERNAL'S VENGEANCE

MY lords, Tristan was long in the wood and he suffered much hardship there. He dared not remain in one place. He did not lie at night in the place where he rose in the morning. He knew that the king was making a search for him and that a proclamation had been made throughout the land that whoever found him was to capture him. They were very short of bread in the wood, they lived on flesh and nothing else. How could they help losing their colour? Their clothes were ragged, for branches tore them. They were a long time in the forest of Morrois. Each of them was suffering equal hardship, but neither was distressed on the other's account. Yseut feared that Tristan might repent for her sake; and for his part Tristan deeply regretted that there was discord between Yseut and Mark because of him, and he too feared that she might repent of her folly.

Hear now what happened one day to one of the three villains – may God curse them! – who exposed the lovers. He was a rich man and much esteemed, and he took great interest in dogs. The Cornish people were so afraid of the forest of Morrois that not one dared enter it. They had good cause to be afraid, for if Tristan had captured them he would have hanged them on a tree. They all avoided the forest. One day Governal was with his horse beside a brook which ran down from a little spring. He had taken the saddle off his horse and it was grazing on the fresh grass. Tristan was lying in a bower and the queen, for whom he was suffering such hardship and distress, was held tight in his arms. They had both gone to sleep. From his place of concealment Governal heard the noise of hunting dogs, chasing a stag at great speed. These were the dogs which belonged to one of the three whose plotting had made the king quarrel with the queen. The dogs were in pursuit of the running stag. Governal went along a path to an open space where he could see in the distance the man whom he knew his lord hated more than any other coming along on his own without a squire. He clapped spurs to his horse to urge it on and smacked its neck with his stick. The horse stumbled over a stone. Governal hid beside a tree, waiting for the man who was coming rapidly towards him and was to go slowly away.

No man can turn aside his fate. The villain was not on his guard against revenge for the harm he had done Tristan. Under the tree Governal saw him coming and awaited him eagerly. He said to himself that he would rather let his ashes be scattered to the winds than not take vengeance. For because of that villain and his actions they were all condemned to death. The dogs went away after the fleeing stag and the squire followed the dogs. Governal sprang out of his ambush, remembering the harm this man had done, cut him to pieces with his sword and carried the head away. When the hunters who were pursuing the stag came up they saw their lord's headless body under the tree and turned and ran as fast as they could. They thought this had been done by Tristan, about whom the king had issued the proclamation. It was told throughout Cornwall that one of the three who had brought Tristan into conflict with the king had lost his head. Everyone was frightened and dismayed, and after that they left the wood in peace, only going there rarely to hunt. From the moment a man entered the wood, even for hunting, he was afraid of meeting the fierce Tristan, who was feared on the plains and in the wood.

Tristan was lying in the bower. It was warm and the ground was strewn with leaves. He had gone to sleep and did not know that the man who would have had him killed had lost his life – he was happy when he did know! Governal came to the bower holding the dead man's head in his hands. He tied it by the hair to a fork in the branches. Tristan awoke, saw the head, started with fear and leaped to his feet. His master cried:

'Do not move, you are safe! I have killed him with my sword. This man was your enemy.'

Tristan was very glad of this, for now the man he most feared had been killed. Fear of the forest spread throughout the land and no one dared enter it. Now the lovers had the wood to themselves. While they were in the wood Tristan invented a bow which he called 'Fail Not'. He set it up in the wood in such a way that he found nothing he could not kill. When a stag or deer ran through the wood and touched the branches where the bow was set and stretched, if it knocked the bow high up it was struck high up itself, and if it knocked the bow low down it was as quickly struck low down. When Tristan made the bow he rightfully gave it that name for it never missed anything, high or low, and it was very useful to them for it provided them with many large stags for food. They had to support themselves on game in the wood. They had no more bread and they dared not venture on to the plains. For a long time he hunted like this and it was a wonderful resource, for they had plenty of venison.

My lords, it was a summer's day at harvest-time, not long after Pentecost. The birds were singing at dawn as the dew was falling. Tristan girded on his sword and went alone out of the bower where they had slept. He looked first at the bow 'Fail not', then went into the wood to hunt. Before he came into the wood, had he

known such great suffering? Had anyone ever suffered
so much? But neither Tristan nor Yseut felt this for they
were able to give each other comfort. Never did two
people have as much pleasure as they did while they were
in the wood. Nor, as the story says where Beroul saw it
written down, did two people ever love each other so
much nor pay for it so dearly. The queen rose to greet
Tristan on his return. The heat was so great that day that
it troubled them. Tristan embraced her and said:

'I will rest awhile from hunting.'

'My love, where have you been?'

'After a stag which has tired me out. I chased it for
so long I am aching all over. I am tired, I want to
sleep.'

The bower was made of green branches with foliage
in places, and the ground was well covered with leaves.
First Yseut lay down; then Tristan drew his sword, put
it between their bodies and lay down himself. Yseut was
wearing her tunic – if she had been naked that day dread-
ful harm would have come to them – and Tristan kept his
trousers on. The queen had on her finger the gold wedd-
ing ring set with emeralds that the king had given her. Her
finger was woefully thin, the ring all but slipping off.
Hear how they were lying: she had put one arm under
Tristan's neck and the other, I think, over him; her
arms were clasped tightly around him. Tristan in his
turn had his arms around her, for their affection was not
feigned. Their mouths were close together, yet there was
a space between them and their bodies were not touching.
There was no wind and the leaves were still. A ray of
sunlight fell on Yseut's face where it shone like glass. So

the lovers went to sleep, not thinking of any harm that might befall them. They were alone in that part of the country for Governal, I think, had gone on horseback to see a forester some way off in the wood.

10

MARK'S DISCOVERY OF THE LOVERS

LISTEN, my lords, to an adventure which should have been dire and dreadful for the lovers! A forester had found the bower where they had slept and was coming through the wood. He followed their tracks until he reached the place where Tristan had made his abode. He saw the sleeping pair and recognized them. He was very frightened and turned pale. He hurried away in fright. He knew that if Tristan woke up he would not be able to give him any pledges and would leave his head behind – no wonder he fled! He ran out of the wood at an astonishing pace. Tristan was asleep with his beloved and they nearly met their deaths. From the exact place where they were sleeping I believe it was two good leagues to where the king held his court. The forester ran quickly because he had heard the proclamation made about Tristan that whoever reported truly about him to the king would be given a large reward. The forester kept this in mind and ran swiftly. King Mark was holding an assembly of his barons in his palace and the hall was filled. The forester came down the hill and went up to the palace. Do you think he dared stop before he reached the steps of the hall? He entered the hall. The king saw the forester running in so quickly and called to him at once:

'Are you bringing news in such a hurry? You look like a man running with dogs that are pursuing their prey. Do you want to make a complaint here about someone? If you want something tell me your message. Has someone refused to give you your money, or chased you out of my forest?'

'Please listen to me, king, for a moment. It has been proclaimed in Cornwall that if anyone finds your nephew he should either risk his life to take him prisoner or come to tell you. I have found him, but I fear your anger. If I tell you will you kill me? I can lead you to where he is asleep with the queen. I saw him a short while ago, I believe they were fast asleep. I was very frightened when I saw them.'

The king heard him and sighed deeply, for he was dismayed and very angry. He whispered to the forester: 'Where are they? Tell me!'

'In a bower in the Morrois. They are sleeping in each other's arms. Come quickly and we shall be avenged on them. King, if you do not take a cruel vengeance, you have beyond doubt lost your right to rule this land.'

The king said to him: 'Go outside. As you hold your body dear, tell no one, stranger or friend, what you know. At the Croiz Rouge, at the side of the road near the cemetery, you are to wait for me without stirring. I shall give you as much gold and silver as you want, I promise you.'

The forester left the king and went to the Croiz where

he sat down. (May he be blinded, for he tried so hard to harm Tristan! It would have been better for him if he had taken himself off for he afterwards died a wretched death, as you will hear later in the story.) The king went into his chamber and sent for all his trusted men. He forbade them to come one step after him. They all said:

'King, is this a jest, to go somewhere alone? There has never been a king who has not always taken great care of himself. What news have you heard? Do not go anywhere on the word of a spy.'

The king replied: 'I have received no news, but a girl has sent for me to come quickly. She expressly asks me not to take a companion. I shall go quite alone on horse without a companion or a squire.'

They said: 'We are sorry to hear this. Cato ordered his son to avoid solitary places.'

'I know this well enough. Leave me now to do what I want to.'

The king had his horse saddled and girded on his sword. He lamented Tristan's wickedness in taking from him the beautiful Yseut, with whom he had now become a fugitive. The king thought menacingly that he would not fail to do them harm if he found them together. The king was determined to kill them; this was a terrible wrong. He went out of the city saying to himself he would rather be hanged than not take vengeance on those who had caused him so much disgrace. He came to the Croiz where the forester was waiting and told him to go on quickly and lead him straight to where they were. They entered the wood in the shade of the trees. The spy went in front and the king followed him, trusting to the sword at his side with which he had struck many good blows. He was acting too presumptuously, for if Tristan were to wake up and the nephew were to fight the uncle, the battle could not end before one was dead. King Mark told the forester he would give him twenty silver marks if he led him quickly to the place where he intended committing this folly. The forester – may he be shamed! – said they were nearing their destination. The spy made the king dismount from his good Gascon horse and ran to the other side to hold the stirrup. They tied the horse's reins to a branch of a green apple-tree. They went a little further and saw the bower they were heading for. The king undid the clasps of fine gold on his cloak; with his cloak off he had a fine body. He drew his sword from its scabbard and went forward angrily, saying to himself that he would die if he did not kill them now. He entered the bower with his sword in his hand. The forester followed him in and hurried after the king, but the king motioned him back. In anger the king raised his sword, but then his anger left him: the blow was never to fall on them, and it would have been a great sorrow if he had killed them. For he saw that she was wearing her tunic, that there was a space between them and their mouths were not joined. And he saw the naked sword between them which kept them apart and the trousers that Tristan was wearing.

'God,' said the king, 'what can this be? Now I have seen their way of life so clearly that, by God, I do not know what to do, whether to kill them or draw back. They have been here in the wood for a long time. I can well believe, if I have any sense, that if they loved each other wickedly they would certainly not be wearing clothes and there would be no sword between them. They would be lying together quite differently. I was intent on killing them, but now I shall not touch them, I shall curb my anger. They have no mind for a wicked love. I shall not strike either of them. They are asleep: if I laid my hands on them I should be doing them too great a wrong. And if I wake this sleeping pair and he kills me or I kill him, there will be ugly talk. I shall give them a sign before they wake up so that they will know for certain that someone found them asleep and took pity on them, and that neither I nor anyone in my kingdom is in any way seeking their death. I can see the precious emerald ring on the queen's finger which I gave her, and I have one here which was hers. I shall take mine from her finger. I have a pair of fur gloves with me which she brought from Ireland. I shall cover up the ray of sunlight shining on her face, I think it is burning her. When I come to leave I shall take from between them the sword which split Morholt's head.'

The king unfastened his gloves and looked at the sleeping pair. With the gloves he kindly shielded Yseut from the ray of sunlight. He saw the ring on her finger and drew it off so gently that the finger did not move. Formerly it had been hard to put on, but now her fingers were so thin that it slipped off easily. The king slid it off very carefully. He gently took the sword from between them and put his own in its place. He went out of the bower, came to his horse and leaped on its back. He told the forester to take himself off and they both departed. The king went away and left them sleeping. This time he did nothing else, and went back to his city. Several people asked him where he had been for so long. But he lied in answer and no one knew where he had gone nor what he had done.

But now hear of the two lovers whom the king had left sleeping in the wood. The queen dreamed that she was in a richly hung tent in a great forest. Towards her came two lions who wanted to devour her. She wanted to call for mercy but the lions, both famished, each took her by the hand. In her fear Yseut cried out and woke up. The white fur gloves fell on to her breast. Tristan woke up at the cry he heard, his whole face flushed. In his fright he leaped up and snatched his sword. He looked at the blade and could not see the notch. Then he saw the gold pommel and knew that it was the king's sword. The queen saw on her finger the ring she had given him and knew that hers had been taken from her finger. She cried:

'Mercy, my lord! The king has found us here!'

He answered: 'My lady, it is true. We did him a great wrong and now we shall have to leave the Morrois. He has taken my sword and left me his own. He could surely have killed us.'

'Truly, my lord, I think so too.'

'My love, there is nothing for it now but flight. He has gone away, hoping that will deceive us. He was alone and he has gone back for more men. I am sure he intends to capture us. My lady, let us flee towards Wales, I am beginning to feel faint.'

Tristan went pale. Their squire came back and led the horse in. He saw that his master was pale and asked what was the matter:

'By my faith, master, King Mark found us here while we were asleep. He left his sword and has taken mine away. I fear he is plotting some treachery. He took the fine ring on Yseut's finger and left his own. By this exchange, master, we can see that he wants to deceive us. For he was alone when he found us, fear gripped him and he went away. He has gone back for men, and he has many fierce and spirited warriors. He will lead them here, for he wants to kill me and Queen Yseut. He wants to capture us, burn us and scatter our ashes in the sight of the Cornish people. Let us flee, we must not delay.'

They had no cause to delay. If they were afraid, they could not help it: they knew the king was wicked and violent. They rode away in great haste, they feared the king because of what had happened. They crossed the Morrois and went on, fear made them cover great distances in a day. They were heading for Wales. Their love will yet cause them much hardship. For three full years they had suffered greatly, their flesh had grown pale and limp.

II

THE LOVE POTION

MY lords, you have heard of the wine they drank which caused them to suffer greatly for so long. But you do not know, I think, the duration of the efficacy of the love-drink, the wine mixed with herbs: Yseut's mother, who brewed it, made it for three years of love. She made it for

Mark and her daughter; another tasted it and suffered because of this. For as long as the three years lasted the potion had such power over Tristan and the queen that each of them could say:

'I am not weary.'[2]

The day after St John's day the three years to which the potion was limited came to an end. Tristan had risen from his bed, Yseut remained in the bower. Tristan took aim at a stag and shot an arrow that pierced its side. The stag fled and Tristan gave chase. He followed it until evening. As he was running after the beast, it came to the very hour when he had drunk the love potion, and he stopped. Instantly he began to repent, and said to himself:

'God, I have had so much hardship! For fully three years today there has not been a moment when I was not suffering, either on a feast-day or a week-day. I have forgotten chivalry and the life of a knight at court. I am an exile in this country and there is nothing left of the light and grey furs I had. I am not in the company of the knights at court. God, how dearly my uncle would love me if I had not caused him so much distress. God, how badly things are going for me! I ought now to be at the court of a king with a hundred squires in attendance, preparing to win their spurs and enter my service. I ought to go to another land where I could fight battles to win rewards. And it grieves me to think of the queen. I give her a bower of leaves in place of a curtained room. She is in the wood, and she could be living with her servants in fine rooms hung with silken cloths. For my sake she has erred in following this way of life. I call for mercy to God who is Lord of all the world, may he give me the strength to part from my uncle's wife and leave her in peace with him. I swear to God that, if I could, I should willingly arrange for Yseut to be reconciled with King Mark, to whom she was wedded as the Law of Rome prescribes, as many good men witnessed.'

Tristan leaned on his bow and regretted many times the great wrong he had done King Mark in causing him to be estranged from his wife. Tristan lamented much that evening. Hear now how Yseut felt. She said to herself:

'Alas, poor wretch, why were you given youth? You are here in the wood like a slave, you can find few people to serve you. I am a queen, but I lost that name through the potion which we drank on the sea. It was Brangain's fault, for the potion was in her guard. Alas, she guarded it so badly! She could do nothing about it afterwards for it was too grave a mistake. I ought to have around me in my rooms the damsels of the kingdom and the daughters of the free vassals, and I should be arranging good marriages for them with noblemen. Tristan, the person who brought us the love potion to drink led us sadly astray; we could not have been more deceived.'

Tristan said to her: 'Noble queen, we are wasting our youth. Fair friend, if I could find a way to be reconciled with King Mark, if he would forgo his anger and accept our affirmation that never at any time, in deed or word, did I love you in a way that would shame him, then there is no knight in his kingdom, from Lidan to Durham, who would not find me armed in the field if he dared to say that I loved you dishonourably. And if it was Mark's wish, when you made this defence, to allow me to remain in his household, I should serve him with honour as my uncle and my lord. No warrior in his land would give him better support in war. But if he wished to take you back and not accept my service, I should go to the king of Dumfries or to Brittany with no companion except Governal. Noble queen, wherever I might be I would always be at your service. I should not seek this separation if we could remain together, and if it were not that because of me you have suffered and still are suffering in this wilderness. Because of me you have lost the name of queen. You would now be in a place of honour with the king at court if it were not for the potion that was given us at sea. Noble, lovely Yseut, advise me what to do.'

'May Jesus be thanked, my lord, that you are willing to give up this life of sin! Do you remember the hermit Ogrin who preached to us and told us so much of Holy Writ when we were at his dwelling at the edge of the wood? Fair sweet friend, if your heart has indeed turned to repentance, nothing could be better. Let us hurry back to him. I am sure he will give us good counsel through which we may still reach eternal joy.'

Tristan listened and gave a sigh: 'Noble queen, let us go back to the hermitage. With the help of Friar Ogrin we shall be able, tonight or in the morning, to send our message to King Mark in a letter, without needing to visit him.'

'Tristan, well said! Let us both pray that the King of Heaven will have mercy on us, Tristan, my love!'

12

THE HERMIT OGRIN. II

THEY turned back into the wood and walked on until they reached the hermitage. They found the hermit Ogrin reading, and when he saw them he gave them a friendly greeting. They sat down in his chapel.

'Exiles, what great suffering love forces on you! How long will this madness last? You have been leading this life for too long, and I beg you to repent.'

Tristan said to him: 'Now listen: if we have led this life for a long time, such was our destiny. For three full years now, if I do not err, we have never been free of suffering. If we can find a way to reconcile the queen and King Mark I shall never again seek to be in the king's household. Instead I shall go away within a month to Brittany or Lyoness. But if my uncle will allow me to serve him at his court then I shall serve him loyally. Sir, my uncle is a great king. [We are seeking his forgiveness.] Tell us what you think will be best to do from what you have heard and we shall do as you say.'

My lords, hear of the queen. She fell at the hermit's feet and was not slow to beg his help in reconciling them with the king. She said sorrowfully: 'Never for the rest of my life shall I have any thoughts of wickedness. You understand that I am not saying I repent on Tristan's account nor that I do not love him honourably and without shame as a friend. But our physical intercourse is now at an end.'

The hermit wept as she spoke and gave thanks to God for what he had heard: 'God, Almighty King, I thank you from my heart that you have let me live long enough for these two people to come to seek my counsel about their sins. I am deeply thankful to You. By my faith and my religion, I swear that you shall have good advice from me. Tristan, listen to me for a while now that you have come here to my dwelling. And you, queen, hear my words and mark them well. When a man and woman sin, if they have first loved each other and then given up their sin, and if they become penitent and make true repentance, God will pardon their misdeed, however horrible or ugly it is. Tristan, queen, listen to me carefully: to escape the shame and to cover up the wrong we shall have to think of some suitable falsehoods. You have asked for my advice and you shall have it now. I can cut up some parchment to make a letter which we shall send. At the head it will bear greetings from you. Send it to Lantyan with your greetings to the king and say that you are in the wood with the queen and that if he would forgo his anger and take the queen back you would do as much for him and would go to his court. Tell the king that you would let him hang you if there was anyone at his court, a wise man or a fool, who was so hardy that you could not defend yourself against him if he accused you of loving the queen dishonourably. Tristan, I make bold to give you that advice because you will never find a knight there who would dare take up your challenge. I give you this advice in good faith. The king cannot gainsay that when he wanted to put you to death by burning because of the dwarf he would not hear your defence – both the

barons and the people are witness. It was the mercy of
God that allowed you to escape, it is well known, for had
it not been for God's might you would have been shame-
fully killed when you made a leap that would frighten any
man from Costentin to Rome. Then you fled in fear. You
rescued the queen and since then you have been together
in the forest. You took her from her own land to give to
him in marriage. All that was done, he well knows. He
was married in Lantyan. You could not have failed her
and you preferred to flee with her. If he is willing to
accept your defence in the presence of his barons and his
people, you will offer to make your defence at his court.
When your loyalty to him is re-affirmed let him take back
his noble wife, if it is his wish and if his vassals consent.
And if you knew that it would not displease him, you
would gladly be a warrior in his service. But if he will not
accept that, you will cross the sea to Dumfries and go to
serve another king. Such will the letter be.'

'I agree. But, with your permission, Father Ogrin, let
it be added to the parchment that I dare not trust him.
He offered a reward for my head. But I beg him, as a
lord I truly love, to write a letter in answer containing
all his wishes. I wish his letter to be affixed to the Croiz
Rouge on the heath. I dare not tell him where I am; I fear
he would try to capture me. But I will trust his letter. I
will do whatever he wishes. Master, let my letter be sealed.
At the end write *Vale*. I have nothing more to add.'

The hermit Ogrin took pen, ink and parchment and
wrote all the words down. When he had done this he took
a ring and pressed its stone into the wax. The letter was
sealed and the hermit handed it to Tristan.

'Who will carry it?' said the hermit.

'I shall.'

'Tristan, do not say so!'

'Certainly Father, I shall take it. I know Lantyan well. If you are agreeable, Father Ogrin, the queen will remain here. Soon, when it is dark and the king is sound asleep, I shall go with my squire on horseback. There is a hill outside the town. I shall dismount there and go forward on foot. My squire will guard my horse – no priest or layman ever saw a better.'

After sunset that night, when it had grown quite dark, Tristan set off with his squire. He knew the lie of the land well. They rode to Lantyan. He dismounted and went into the town. The watchmen were giving loud blasts on their horns. Tristan slipped into a ditch and went along it until he reached the hall of the castle. He was in great danger. He came to the window of the king's chamber and called him, taking care not to speak too loud. The king awoke and said:

'Who are you, coming at this time? What do you want? Tell me your name.'

'Sire, I am Tristan. I am bringing a letter for you which I will leave on this window ledge. I dare not talk to you for long. I am leaving the letter behind, I dare not stay.'

Tristan turned to leave. The king sprang out of bed and called out three times: 'For God's sake, fair nephew, wait for your uncle!'

The king picked up the letter. Tristan had gone. He dared not remain and slipped away quickly back to his waiting squire and jumped on his horse.

Governal said: 'Madman, hurry up! Let us go along the side roads.'

They went through the wood and at daybreak they reached the hermitage. Ogrin was praying with all his strength to the Heavenly King to watch over Tristan and Governal. When he saw them, how happy he was! He gave thanks to his Creator. There was no need to ask if Yseut had feared for them. Her eyes had been full of tears from the time they left the previous evening until she and the hermit saw them again. It had seemed to her a very long time. When she saw them coming she begged them to tell her where they had been. [Tristan said they had been to Lantyan but] nothing was said of what he did there.

'Tristan, tell me, as God loves you, have you been to the king's court?'

And Tristan recounted everything: how he had been to the city and spoken to the king, how the king had called him back, and how he had left the letter and the king had found it.

'God,' said Ogrin, 'I give You thanks. Tristan, you may be sure that you will shortly have a letter from King Mark.'

Tristan laid down his bow. They all stayed in the hermitage.

The king awoke his household. First he sent for his chaplain and handed him the letter. The chaplain broke the seal and looked at it. At the head of the letter he read Tristan's greetings to the king. The chaplain soon finished reading the letter and told the king its contents. The king listened and was greatly pleased, for he loved his wife very much. The king awoke all his barons and sent especially for those who were most worthy. When they were all assembled the king spoke and they fell silent.

'My lords, a letter has been delivered to me here. I am your king and you are my marquises. Let the letter be read and listened to. When it has been read, I beg you to give me your counsel. You must advise me well.'

Dinas was the first to rise, and he addressed his peers: 'Hear me, my lords! If you do not hear me speak well now, never believe anything I say. If anyone has better things to say, let him do so, and may his words be wise. We do not know where the letter has been sent from. Let it be read first of all, and then according to its contents let anyone who can give good advice do so. I declare that anyone who gives his rightful lord bad advice can do no greater wrong.'

The Cornish barons said to the king: 'Dinas has spoken like a true vassal. Sir chaplain, read the letter from beginning to end in the presence of us all.'

The chaplain opened out the letter and stood before the king: 'Now listen carefully, my lords. Tristan, the king's nephew, first sends greetings and love to the king and all his barons. "Sire, remember well your marriage with the king of Ireland's daughter. I crossed the sea to Ireland and I won her by my prowess. I killed the huge, crested dragon, for which she was given to me. I brought her to your country, sire, where you took her to wife, as all your knights saw. You had not long been together before the evil tongues in your kingdom began to make you believe their lies. I am quite ready to give this challenge to anyone who would accuse her: I will defend her, fair sire, against any man on foot or on horseback – each one to have weapons and a horse. I say that she never had a wrongful love for me nor I for her. If I cannot defend her and exculpate myself at your court, then I will make my defence in front of your army. I make exception of none of your barons who would seek to harm me and have me condemned to be burnt. You know, sire, fair uncle, that you wanted in your wrath to burn us. But God had pity on us and we worship Him for this. By good fortune the queen escaped. This was just, may God save me, for you were very wrong in wanting to put her to death. I escaped by leaping over a high cliff. Then the queen was given to the lepers as her punishment. I rescued her from them and carried her off. Since then I have always been with her. I could not fail her when she had been condemned to death for my sake. Since then we have stayed in the wood for I was not rash enough to show myself in the open [after you had issued a proclamation that anyone who could should] capture us and hand us over to you. You would have had us burned or hanged. Because of that we had to flee. But if it were now your pleasure to take back Yseut the Fair, no baron in this land would serve you better than I. But if you are advised differently and will not accept my service, I shall go to the King of Dumfries. I shall go overseas and you will never hear of me again. Think carefully, king, over what you have heard. I can no longer suffer this torment: either I shall be reconciled with you or I shall take the king's daughter back to Ireland where I brought her from. She shall be queen in her own country."' The chaplain said to the king: 'Sire, that is the end of the letter.'

The barons heard this request and Tristan's offer to do battle with them for the sake of the king of Ireland's daughter. There was not a baron of Cornwall who did not say:

'King, take back your wife. The men whose accusations of the queen we have just been reminded of acted unwisely. But we cannot advise you to allow Tristan to remain on this side of the sea. Let him go to the rich king of Galway who is at war with the Scots king. He can remain there and you will hear news of him and you can send for him later. Otherwise we shall not know where he has gone. Send him a letter saying he is to bring the queen here soon.'

The king called his chaplain and said: 'Let this letter be written quickly. You have heard what to put in it. Hurry with the letter. I am very anxious, I have not seen Yseut the Fair for a long time. She has suffered greatly in her youth. When the letter is sealed, take it and affix it to the Croiz Rouge. Let it be taken there this very night. Send greetings from me.'

When the chaplain had written the letter, he took it and affixed it to the Croiz Rouge. Tristan did not sleep that night. Before midnight came he had crossed the Blanche Lande and taken the sealed letter; he knew that part of Cornwall well. He came back with the letter and gave it to Ogrin, who read the generous words of the king, who was willing to forgo all his anger towards Yseut and would gladly take her back; and he read when the reconciliation was to take place.

'The king will speak to you then as he must do, like a man who truly believes in God. Tristan, what joy for you! Your request that the king should take back the queen has been given a speedy hearing. All his people have advised him to do this. But they dared not advise him to retain you in his service; instead you should go to another land to serve a king who is engaged in war and remain there a year or two. If the king then so wishes, you may return to him and Yseut. In three days from now the king will be ready to receive her, without any treachery on his part. The meeting between you and them will be at the Gué Aventurous, where you will hand Yseut over and she will be received. There is nothing more in the letter.'

'God,' said Tristan, 'what sorrow it is to part! How unhappy is the man who loses his beloved! But it must be done to make up for all the suffering you have endured on my account; you need suffer no longer. When the time comes to take leave of each other I will pledge my love to you and you shall pledge yours to me. Whatever land I am in, neither peace nor war will prevent me from sending my news to you. And send me your greetings, my love.'

Yseut sighed deeply and spoke: 'Tristan, listen a moment: leave me Husdant, your dog. No hunter ever looked after his dog with such care as I shall, my fair friend. When I see the dog, I think I shall often remember you; I shall never be so unhappy that seeing him will not make me cheerful again. Never, since the time when God's Law was first given to man, was any animal so well tended or given such a fine bed as he shall have. Tristan, my love, I have a ring with a green jasper mounted: fair friend, for my sake wear the ring on your finger. And if you wish to send a messenger to me, I assure you I shall believe nothing unless I see this ring. No king will forbid me, once I see this ring, from doing whatever I am asked to, whether it be wisdom or folly, by the man who bears this ring; provided only that it is to our honour. This I promise you in true love. My love, will you let me have Husdant over there as a gift?'

He replied: 'I will give you Husdant for love.'

'You are very kind. Now that you have given me the dog, take the ring as your reward.'

She took it from her finger and put it on his. Then each kissed the other to signify possession of the gifts.

13

YSEUT'S RETURN TO KING MARK

THE hermit went to St Michael's Mount because of all the fine goods that can be found there. He bought bright and dark clothes, silks of deep purple, fine woollen material, linen whiter than a lily, and a gentle palfrey with trappings of shining gold. Ogrin the hermit bought so much – some for cash, some on credit and some by bargaining – that the queen would be richly clad in all the light and dark-coloured silks and ermine. It was proclaimed over the whole of Cornwall that the king was to be reconciled with his wife: 'The reconciliation between us will take place at the Gué Aventurous.' The news was heard everywhere and no knight or lady hesitated to come to the gathering. They had a great longing to see the queen, for she was loved by everyone, except the villains – may God destroy them! All four of them had their just deserts: two were killed by the sword, the third by an arrow; they met their deaths in their own country. And the forester who betrayed the lovers also met a cruel death, for the noble and fair Perinis killed him afterwards in the wood with a sling. God avenged them on all these four, for He humbles arrogant pride.

My lords, on the day of the meeting King Mark was attended by a great number of people. Many pavilions had been erected and many barons had set up tents; they covered a large part of the meadow. Tristan rode beside his love until they came to the boundary stone. Under his tunic he was wearing a hauberk, for he was greatly afraid on account of the wrong he had done King Mark. He saw the tents in the meadow and recognized the king and his attendants. He called to Yseut and said tenderly:

'My lady, keep Husdant. I beg you, for God's sake, to look after him. If you ever loved him, love him now. There is the king, your lord, with the men of his kingdom. We shall not be able to speak together for much longer now. I can see the knights and the king and his soldiers coming towards us. For the sake of our glorious God, if I send you a message either soon or later, carry out my wishes, my lady!'

'Listen to me, Tristan my love: by the faith I owe you, if you do not send me that ring on your finger I shall not believe anything a messenger says. But as soon as I see that ring, no tower, wall or fortress shall stop me from doing straight away whatever my lover requires, if it is honourable and loyal and I know it is your wish.'

'God bless you, my lady,' said Tristan, and he drew her towards him and embraced her. Yseut was not unwise, and she said:

'My love, attend to what I have to say. You will do well to listen to me. You have brought me here to be returned to the king by the advice of Ogrin – I wish him well. I beg you, for God's sake, my fair sweet love, not to leave this land until you know how the king is going to behave towards me, for he may be angry or uneasy. When the king has taken me back I beg you, as one who loves you dearly, to stay with the forester Orry. May it not grieve you to stay there for my sake! We lay there many a night in the bed which he made for us. [I am afraid of the king's wicked barons.] Those three who caused us trouble will come to harm in the end, their dead bodies will yet lie in the wood. My love, I fear them – may Hell open and swallow them up! I fear them because they are evil men. You can stay in that good cellar under the forester's hut. I will send you news from court through Perinis. My love, may God honour you, and may it not distress you to stay there! You will see my messenger often. I will tell you my news through my servant and your squire.'

'It will not distress me at all, my dear love. If anyone reproaches you for your folly, he will have to reckon with me as his enemy.'

'Many thanks, my lord!' said Yseut. 'I feel much

happier now, you have reassured me that everything will go well.'

They advanced far enough to exchange greetings with those who were coming towards them. The king came proudly forward, a bow-shot in front of his men; with him was Dinas of Dinan. Tristan was holding the queen's rein as he led her. He gave the king a formal salutation:

'King, I hereby restore to you the noble Yseut. No man ever made a better restitution. I see the men of your land here: in their hearing I want to request you to allow me to clear myself and make my defence in your court. Never at any time did she or I love each other wickedly. You have been led to believe lies; but, as God gives me joy and happiness, they never put it to the test in a combat on foot or otherwise. If I agree to this taking place in your court, then burn me in sulphur if I am found guilty! If I can come safe through the ordeal, let no one, long-haired or bald, [ever accuse us again. If it is your wish,] retain me in your service; otherwise I shall go to Lyoness.'

The king spoke to his nephew. Andret, who was born in Lincoln, said to him: 'King, retain him, men will fear you the more.'

The king's heart softened and he all but agreed to this. He drew Andret to one side and left the queen with Dinas, who was true and loyal and who always acted honourably. He laughed and talked with the queen and helped her take off the rich woollen cloak round her neck. She was wearing a tunic over a long silk gown. How could I describe her mantle? The hermit who bought it never regretted its high price! She was wearing rich clothes over her noble body, and her eyes shone beneath her glinting hair. The seneschal was happy to be talking with her. This distressed the three barons – may they be cursed, the evil men! – and they quickly went over to the king.

'Sire,' they said, 'listen to us, we shall give you good advice. The queen was accused and she fled from your domain. If they are together again at court people will say, it seems to us, that you are consenting to their wickedness; there will be few who do not say this. Let Tristan stay away from your court. When a year has passed and you are sure Yseut is faithful to you, then send for Tristan to come. We give you this advice in good faith.'

The king replied: 'Whatever anyone says, I shall always listen to your counsel.'

The barons drew back and on the king's behalf announced his decision. When Tristan heard that there was to be no reprieve for him and that the king wanted him to depart, he took his leave of the queen; each looked at the other affectionately. The queen was blushing, she was ashamed in front of the gathering. Tristan departed; many hearts were made heavy on that day. The king asked where he would go and said he would give him whatever he wanted. He offered him gold and silver and rich clothing.

Tristan answered: 'King of Cornwall, I will never take a farthing from you. I am going off now, as gladly as I can, to the king who is now at war.'

Tristan was handsomely escorted by the king and his barons as he made his way to the sea. Yseut followed him with her eyes and did not move for as long as she could see him. Tristan went on and those who were accompanying him only for a short way turned back; but Dinas stayed beside him. He embraced Tristan often and begged him to be sure to come back to them; the two pledged their mutual trust.

'Dinas, listen to me for a moment: I am departing from here, and you know very well why. If I send Governal to you for anything I need urgently, give it to him, for you owe this to me.'

They kissed each other many times. Dinas begged him to have no fear and to send on all his wishes and he would do everything. Tristan said that he had parted from a lovely woman and swore that he would one day have her with him again, although the king would not allow this. Then Tristan left Dinas, and both were sad at the parting.

Dinas rejoined the king who was waiting for him on the heath. Then the barons rode back to the city at a gallop. All the townspeople came out to meet them, there were more than four thousand men, women and children, all making great joy for Tristan's sake as well as Yseut's. In the city the church bells were ringing. When they heard that Tristan had been sent away there was not a single person who was not saddened. But they were very happy to see Yseut and went to great lengths to show their pleasure: not a street that was not covered over with silk cloth; if there was no silk, tapestry was hung out. Wherever the queen was to walk the road was well strewn. They went along the main road up to the church of St Samson. The queen went there together with all the barons. The bishop came out to meet her with his clerks, monks and abbots, all wearing albs and copes. The queen dismounted and put on a dark blue cloak. The bishop took her hand and conducted her into the church and up to the altar. The brave Dinas, a fine baron, brought her a garment worth fully a hundred silver marks, made of silk richly embroidered with gold: no count or king ever had such a garment. Queen Yseut took it and with a good heart laid it on the altar. It was afterwards made into a chasuble, which only leaves the church treasury on great annual feasts. Those who have seen it say it is still in St Samson's. Then she left the church; the king, the princes and the counts led her to the lofty palace; that day they made great joy there. The door was closed to no one: whoever wanted to eat there might come, and no one was stinted. Everyone paid honour to Yseut on that day. Never since the day when she was married was she so greatly honoured as on that day. The king freed a hundred serfs, and gave arms and armour to twenty squires whom he knighted. Now hear what Tristan did.

Tristan departed after restoring Yseut to Mark. But he left the main road and took a side track and went along paths and by-ways until he arrived secretly at the forester's dwelling. Orry led him through the concealed entrance to his cellar and found him everything he needed. Orry was wonderfully generous. He caught boars and wild sows in his snares and in his enclosures he trapped great stags and hinds, deer and roe-deer. He was not niggardly with the food and gave plenty to his servants. He lived with Tristan concealed in the cellar. Tristan heard news of his beloved brought by the good squire, Perinis.

14

THE VINDICATION OF YSEUT

HEAR now of the three – may God curse them! They had acted very badly to the king in making him angry with Tristan. Not a full month had passed before King Mark went hunting one day; with him went the traitors. Now hear what they did: on one part of the heath the peasants had burnt a clearing; the king stood there listening to his dogs barking. The three barons came up and addressed the king:

'Sire, listen to us: if the queen has behaved wickedly, she has never exculpated herself. This is spoken of as shameful to you; and the barons of your land have begged you many times to make her defend herself against the accusation of loving Tristan. She must vindicate herself if this is false. Let her decide her own defence, and ask her soon in private when you go to bed. If she will not defend herself, banish her from your kingdom.'

The king reddened as he listened: 'By God! Cornish lords, for a long time now you have continually accused her. This time I hear you accusing her of something you might have done better to keep silent about. Tell me, are you trying to have the queen sent back to Ireland? All of you, what do you want from her? Did not Tristan offer to defend her? And you did not dare take up arms! Through you he has left the country. Now you really astonish me: I have already driven him away; am I now to drive away my wife? A hundred curses on the mouth that told me to send him away! By St Stephen the Martyr, you are pestering me and I am very annoyed. I marvel how you can be so quarrelsome! If he did do wrong, he is now suffering for it. You have no care for what pleases me; while you are here I shall never have peace. By St Tresmor of Cahares, I will give you something to think about: before Tuesday is past – today is Monday – you will see Tristan back!'

The king frightened them so much that they could do nothing but retreat. King Mark said: 'May God destroy you for seeking to shame me like this! It will certainly not do you any good. I will recall the knight you have made me banish.'

When they saw how upset and angry the king was, the three barons left him in the clearing and rode to some waste ground on the heath, where they dismounted. They said to each other:

'What shall we do? King Mark is in a very bad mood. Soon he will send for his nephew, and no vows or promises will stop him doing this. And if Tristan comes back, it is the finish for us, for if he finds any of us three in the wood or on a path he will not fail to spill fresh blood from our bodies. Let us tell the king he will be left in peace now and we shall never again talk to him about it.'

The king had not moved from the middle of the burnt clearing. They went to him but he quickly repelled them, he no longer paid heed to their words. He swore to himself, by God's law, that they had come together for an evil purpose. If he had had the power he would have taken all three prisoner.

'Sire,' they said, 'listen to us: you are angry and resentful because we have spoken to you about your honour. It is right that a man should advise his lord, yet we have gained your ill will. Cursed be the man who hates you, however strong a knight he is. He would certainly be harshly treated by you and he would go away. But we are faithful to you and we give you loyal advice. If you do not believe us, then do as you will and we shall certainly keep silent. Do not be angry with us.'

The king listened, saying nothing. He leaned on his saddle-bow and said, without turning his head towards them:

'My lords, it is still only a short time ago that you heard my nephew's vindication of my wife; you would not take up your weapons. Go away now on foot. I forbid you from now on to make any strife; leave my land. By St Andrew, whom men seek across the sea in Scotland, you have planted a pain in my heart which will not leave me for a year. For your sake I have banished Tristan.'

Before the king stood the felons, Godwin, Ganelon and the wicked Denoalan; all three addressed him together, but he would not listen. Without staying any longer the king went away. And with evil thoughts the three barons left. They had strong well-defended castles situated on cliffs and high hills; they could do their lord much harm if things did not improve. The king did not stay long and did not wait for his dogs or the huntsmen. He rode back to Tintagel to his castle, dismounted and went in. No one saw this or knew what he was doing. He entered his chamber still wearing his sword. Yseut rose to greet him, came up to him and took the sword; then she sat at his feet. He took her by the hand and lifted her up. She looked at him, saw the cruel, angry expression in his face and realized that he was upset.

'Alas,' she whispered, 'my lover has been found, my lord has captured him!'

She spoke softly between her teeth. The blood mounted swiftly to her face and her heart went cold within her. She fell on her back in front of the king in a swoon; her face was ashen. [The king was greatly startled and he bent down] and raised her in his arms, embraced her and kissed her. He thought that some illness had stricken her. When she had recovered from her swoon, he said:

'My dear love, what is the matter?'

'Sire, I am afraid.'

'You have nothing to fear.'

When she heard him reassuring her, her colour returned and she felt better; she was soothed once more. She spoke sweetly to the king:

'Sire, I saw by your face that your huntsmen had upset you; you must not be upset by hunting!'

The king listened to her, laughed and embraced her and said:

'My love, I have three evil barons, who have been here for a long time and who hate my good fortune. If I do not disown them now and banish them from my land the villains will no longer believe in my power. They have tested me enough already and I have given in to them too much: there is no longer any question of changing my mind. Because of the lies they told me I have driven my nephew away. I am no longer paying heed to what they say. My nephew will soon come back and avenge me on the three villains; through him they will yet be hanged.'

The queen heard him and would have spoken out loud but did not dare. She wisely remained calm and said to herself:

'God has worked a miracle here if my lord is angry against the men who first accused me. May God bring them shame!'

She spoke softly so that no one could hear. The fair Yseut, who was wise in speaking, said to the king quite innocently:

'Sire, what evil things have they said about me? Everyone can say what he thinks. I have no protection save you; this is why they are seeking to harm me. May God, our Heavenly Father, curse them! They have made me afraid so often!'

'My lady,' said the king, 'listen to me now: three of my most worthy barons have gone away in anger.'

'Sire, why? What are their reasons?'

'They are accusing you.'

'Of what, sire?'

'I will tell you,' said the king. 'You have not vindicated yourself concerning Tristan.'

'And if I do?'

'And they said to me [it should be done quickly. But I would not believe them, and I did not want to ask you to defend yourself because of all] that they told me.'

'I am ready.'

'When will you do it? This very day?'

'Grant me a short delay.'

'It will be long enough.'

'Sire, for the sake of God and His Holy Name, listen to me and advise me. What can be happening? It is incredible that they do not leave me in peace for a moment! So help me God, I shall make no defence for them except in a way which I shall arrange myself. If I gave my oath, sire, in your court in the presence of your people, three days would not pass before they would be saying that they wanted another defence. Sire, I have no relative in this land who would make war or who would rebel on account of my distress. But I should be perfectly willing to make my defence. I pay no heed to their chatter. If they want me to swear an oath, or if they want a trial by ordeal, let them fix a time – they cannot make any ordeal so harsh that I will not undergo it. At the appointed time and place I will have King Arthur and his household; if I exculpate myself in his presence, then if anyone seeks to calumniate me afterwards, those who have witnessed my defence would come to my protection against any Cornishman or Saxon. For that reason I should be glad if they were there to see my defence with their own eyes. If King Arthur is there, and Gawain his courteous nephew, Gerflet and Kay the Seneschal, the king has a hundred vassals who will not be false concerning what they hear and who would fight against calumnies. Sire, it will be to everyone's advantage if I can make my defence before them. The Cornish are slanderers and treacherous in many ways. Appoint a time and announce that you want everyone, poor and rich, to be at the Blanche Lande. State expressly that you will take away the inheritance of whoever is not there; then you will be finished with them. I am sure in my own mind that as soon as King Arthur hears my message he will come here. I have known his nobility of heart for long.'

The king replied: 'You have spoken well.'

Then a proclamation was made throughout the land and a time fixed for fifteen days hence. The king sent to inform the three Cornish barons who had left his court in anger; they were very pleased, whatever the outcome was to be. Now everyone throughout the land knew the time arranged for the meeting, and that King Arthur was to be there and most of the knights of his household with him. Nor had Yseut been slow: she had sent Perinis to remind Tristan of all the pain and suffering she had undergone for him that year; now she could be compensated for it! With Tristan's help she would be able to live in peace.

'Tell him that there is a marsh he knows at the end of a plank bridge at the Malpas – I once soiled my clothes a little there. Let him stand on the mound at the end of the plank bridge on this side of the Blanche Lande wearing the garments of a leper. He is to carry a wooden drinking-cup tied by a strap to a bottle underneath, with a staff in his other hand. Then let him hear my plan: on the day he is to be seated on the mound; his face will be badly pock-marked. He must hold his cup in front of his face, simply asking for alms from the passers-by. They will give him gold and silver – he is to keep the silver for me until I can see him privately in a quiet room!'

Perinis said: 'My lady, I promise to tell Tristan all

this.' Perinis left the queen. He entered the wood by going through the middle of a copse and went on into the wood all alone. At evening he came to Tristan's hiding-place in the cellar, where they had risen from their meal. Tristan was glad to see him for he knew that the noble squire was bringing him news from his beloved. Each took the other's hand and they sat down on a high seat. Perinis related all the queen's message. Tristan bowed his head and swore an oath that it would be unlucky for the men who had thought of accusing the queen; it could not fail to happen that they would yet lose their heads or hang high on the gallows.

'Give the queen this message, word for word: I shall be there on the day, let her have no fear; let her be gay, healthy and cheerful! I shall not have another bath in hot water until I have taken vengeance with my sword on the men who are causing her so much grief. They have proved themselves to be wicked traitors. Tell her that I have thought of a good way of saving her from the oath. I shall see her soon. Go and tell her not to worry or be afraid, for I shall be at the place of judgement disguised as a beggar. King Arthur will see me sitting at the end of the Malpas but he will not recognize me. I will have alms from him if I can get them. Tell the queen everything I have said to you in this cellar which Orry built so well in stone. And give the queen from me more good wishes than I shall have blemishes on my skin!'

'I shall do that,' said Perinis, and went up the steps. 'Now, my lord, I am going to King Arthur. I have this message to give him: he is to come to hear the queen's oath with a hundred knights who would afterwards be able to protect her if the villains complain in any way about the queen's loyalty. Isn't that a good idea?'

'Now God be with you!'

Perinis went up the remaining steps, mounted his horse and rode away. He did not cease to spur his horse on until he reached Caerleon. He took great trouble in carrying out this errand and he deserved a fine reward. He inquired for news of the king and learned that he was at Stirling. Fair Yseut's squire went along the road which led in that direction. He asked a shepherd who was playing a reed-pipe:

'Where is the king?'

'Sir,' said he, 'he is seated on his throne. You will see the Round Table which turns like the world; his household sits around it.'

'We shall soon be there,' said Perinis. When he arrived at the palace he dismounted beside the stone slab outside and entered quickly. Many sons of counts and sons of rich vassals were there, all serving to win their arms. One of them left his group in a hurry and went up to the king, who called to him:

'Where have you come from?'

'I bring you news: there is a horseman outside seeking you urgently.'

At that moment Perinis came in. Many of the knights watched him as he went up to the king on the dais where all the knights were seated. The squire spoke with assurance:

'God save King Arthur and all his company,' he said, 'from his friend Yseut the Fair!'

The king rose from the table: 'May God in Heaven save

and protect her, and you too, friend! God, I have tried
so hard to get a single message from her! I grant you,
squire, before all my knights, whatever gift you wish.
You and two others shall be made knights, for you bear
a message from the most beautiful woman who could be
found from here to Tudela!'

'Sire,' said Perinis, 'I thank you. Now hear why I
have come, and may your barons please listen too,
especially my lord Gawain. It is no secret that Queen
Yseut has been reconciled with her lord; all the barons
of his kingdom were present when the reconciliation
took place. Tristan offered to clear himself and to defend
the queen against the accusation of disloyalty; but no
one was bold enough to take up arms. Sire, they are
telling King Mark now that he ought to hear her defence.
There is no nobleman of her own family at the king's
court, either French or Saxon, and it is said that a man
can swim more easily when someone supports his chin.
If we are not telling the truth about this, sire, then call
me an idle tale-bearer. The king's mind is not steadfast:
sometimes he thinks one thing, sometimes another.
Fair Yseut told him that she would justify herself only
in your presence. She begs and beseeches you, as your
dear friend, to be at the Gué Aventurous at the appointed
time, and to have a hundred friends with you; may your
court be loyal then and your household sincere. She will
be exculpated before you, and may God take care of her
so that nothing goes wrong! You would then be her
surety, and you would never fail to be her protection in
that matter. The time is set for a week today.'

They all wept profusely; there was not one whose

face was not wet with tears of pity. 'God,' said everyone, 'what are they demanding from her? King Mark does whatever they tell him to, and Tristan is leaving the country. May the man never go to Paradise who will not go to give her the help she deserves, if it is the king's wish!'

Gawain rose to his feet and spoke as a well-taught knight: 'Uncle, if I have your permission, this trial which has been arranged is going to turn out badly for the three villains. The worst of them is Ganelon, I know him well and he knows me. I once forced him into the mire during a rough and strenuous joust. If I get to him, by St Richier, there will be no need for Tristan to come! If I could get my hands on him I would give him very rough treatment and then hang him on top of a hill.'

Gerflet rose after Gawain and went over to take his hand:

'King, the queen has been much hated for a long time by Denoalan, Godwin and Ganelon. May God make me lose my reason if I come up against Godwin and do not pass him through with the blade of my stout ash lance – and may I never kiss another lovely woman beneath the sheets!'

Perinis heard this and bowed towards him.

Evain, the son of Urien, said: 'I know Denoalan well: he thinks of nothing but making accusations and he knows how to make a fool out of the king. I will tell the king this and make him believe me. If I meet him on my way, as I did once, then if he cannot defend himself against me, neither law nor faith will stop me hanging him with my own two hands. The wicked should always be punished. These men mock the king and deceive him.'

Perinis said to King Arthur: 'Sire, I am quite certain that the villains who have caused the queen such harm are now going to suffer for it. No threats have ever been made to your court, even by a man from some distant kingdom, that have not been properly dealt with; all those who deserved it were sad on their departure.'

The king was glad to hear this and he blushed a little:

'Squire, go and eat. These men will see to avenging her.' With great joy in his heart the king addressed his men so that Perinis should hear:

'My noble and honoured men, for this meeting take care that your horses are sleek, your shields and your clothes rich. We shall joust before the beautiful lady of whom you have all just heard news. Any man who hesitates to take up his arms does not greatly value his life!'

The king gave that summons to all of them. They were sorry for the delay – by their wish it would have been the following day.

Hear now of the noble squire. Perinis asked permission to leave. The king mounted his horse Passelande for he wished to accompany the squire. They went along the road talking; all their talk was of the beautiful lady for whom many lances were to be broken. Before their conversation ended the king offered to give Perinis the equipment of a knight; but he would not yet accept it. The king escorted him a little way for the sake of that fair and noble lady, who was full of kindness. They had many things to say as they rode along. The squire had

a fine escort of knights and the noble king. They parted
from each other very unwillingly. The king called to him:

'Go now, fair friend, do not delay. My greetings to
your lady from her loyal servant, and say I am coming to
her to help to make peace. I will do everything she wishes,
for her sake I am eager to, and she will tell me how I can
help her. Remind her of the throwing spear which was
fixed in the post; she will know where that was.[3] Tell
her all this, I beg you.'

'King, you may be sure I shall do so.'

Perinis set spurs to his horse; and the king turned and
rode back. Perinis, who had endured so much in the
queen's service, had delivered his message and now he
rode away. He made his way as fast as he could, not
resting a single day until he reached the place he had
come from. He told Yseut of his journey and she was
very happy to hear from King Arthur and from Tristan.
That night they were at Lidan.

15

YSEUT'S AMBIGUOUS OATH

IT was the tenth night after new moon. What shall I say?
The time was approaching when the queen was to excul-
pate herself. Tristan, her lover, had no qualms about
disguising himself in motley clothes. He wore woollen
garments and no shirt. He wore a rough woollen tunic
and his shoes were patched. He had had made a wide
cloak of coarse wool, which was blackened with smoke.

He had disguised himself extremely well and looked more like a leper than anything else. Nonetheless his sword was tied securely around his waist. Tristan left his lodging secretly and went to Governal, who gave him some advice and said:

'Tristan, my lord, do not do anything foolish. Take care that the queen does not make you any signs of recognition.'

'Master,' he said, 'I shall be careful. Be sure that you do your best for me. Take my shield and my lance and bring them to me with my horse already harnessed. In case I need them, be in hiding near the ford. You know where there is a good crossing, you have known it for a long time. My horse is as white as flour; cover him all over so that he will not be recognized or noticed by anyone. Arthur will be there with all his men and King Mark likewise. The knights from other lands will be jousting to win renown; and for the love of Yseut, I shall myself make a quick sortie. Have the pennant which my love gave me fixed on top of my lance. Go now, master, and I beg you earnestly to do all this with great care.'

Tristan picked up his cup and staff and took farewell of Governal. Governal went to his lodging to get Tristan's armour and did nothing else before he set out. He took care that nobody saw him and went on until he was in hiding near Tristan at the Malpas.

Tristan sat down carelessly on the mound at the end of the marsh. He put his crutch down in front of him; a strap was tied to it and hung around his neck. There was marshy ground all around him. He walked firmly on to the mound. He did not look like a cripple for he was big and well-built; he was not a dwarf, or deformed or hunch-backed. He could hear the people coming and sat down. His face was well covered with bumps. When anyone passed in front of him he would cry out plaintively:

'Woe is me! I never thought I would be a beggar or that I would follow this unhappy calling, but now there is nothing else I can do.'

Tristan made them take out their purses and persevered until everyone gave him something. He took their alms so that no one would say anything. A man might be a pimp for seven years and not be able to get such booty! Even the errand-boys and the humblest of the servants who were eating as they walked along the road Tristan asked for alms for the love of God, as he held his head down. Some gave to him, others struck him. The wretched and cowardly menials called him worthless and a pimp. Tristan heard them and did not answer back; for God's sake, he said, he pardoned them. The peasants were greatly excited and they tried to do him harm, shouting that he was a worthless vagabond (and he was saner than they were!). Tristan chased them away, using his crutch, and made more than fourteen of them bleed so much that they could not staunch the flow of blood. The noble, well-born squires gave him farthings or halfpennies, which he took. He told them that he had to drink always; there was such a great fire in his body that he could hardly cast it out. All those who heard him speak like this began to weep for pity. No one who saw him had the slightest doubt that he was a leper. Then the squires and the servants thought they should hurry on to lodge themselves and set up tents for their lords. There were pavilions of many colours, and no rich man was without his tent. The knights came galloping after them along the roads and paths. There was a great crowd in the marsh and they churned up the soft mud. The horses went in up to their ribs. Many fell in and those who could pulled themselves out. Tristan was not at all dismayed at this, but laughed and called out maliciously to them all:

'Hold your reigns tightly and spur on your horses. For God's sake, use your spurs, the marsh ends ahead of you.'

When they tried to go beyond the marsh, they found that it gave way under their feet. Everyone who went in was covered with mud, and if a man was not wearing boots he was in trouble. The leper stretched out his hand; when he could see someone wallowing in the mud he shook his clapper vigorously. When he saw someone getting deeper in the mud the leper would say:

'Think of me – may God help you out of the Malpas – help me to get new clothes!'

He struck his bowl with his bottle, although this was a strange place to ask for alms. But he did so mischievously so that when his lover, the fair-haired Yseut, passed by she would laugh when she saw it. There was great commotion in the Malpas. All the passers-by soiled their clothes, from far off you could hear the cries of those who were getting dirty in the mud. No one who passed was sure of his way.

At that moment King Arthur came up to see the

crossing with several of his barons; they were afraid of
sinking into the marsh. All the knights of the Round
Table had come to the Malpas with well-groomed horses
and new shields, each bearing his distinctive arms. They
were fully clothed from hands to feet in silk. They were
jousting near the ford. Tristan recognized King Arthur
and called to him:

'King Arthur, sire, I am a sick man, hunch-backed,
a leper, deformed and weak. My father is poor, he never
owned any land. I have come here to seek alms. I have
heard many good things about you, you must not refuse
me. You are wearing fine grey cloth of Regensburg, I
think; under your Rheims linen your skin is white and
smooth; your legs are covered in rich brocade and green
hose, and you have fine woollen gaiters. King Arthur,
can you see how I am scratching myself? Some people
may be hot but I am freezing! For God's sake, let me
have those gaiters!'

The noble king took pity on him. Two squires took
off his gaiters and gave them to the leper, who took them
back quickly to the mound where he sat down again. The
leper spared none of those who passed him by. He was
given many fine clothes as well as King Arthur's gaiters.
Tristan sat down again by the marsh, and as he was
sitting there the proud and powerful King Mark came
towards the mire at a gallop. Tristan began to try to get
something out of him. He made a loud noise with his
clapper and called out with difficulty in a hoarse voice,
breathing heavily through his nose:

'For God's sake, King Mark, a small gift!'

The king drew off his fur hood and said: 'Take it,

brother, and put it on your head. The weather has made you suffer often enough.'

'Sire,' he said, 'thank you! Now you have protected me from the cold.' He put the hood under his cloak, tucked it away and hid it as best he could.

'Where are you from, leper?' asked the king.

'From Caerleon, the son of a Welshman.'

'How many years have you been living away from people?'

'For three years, sire. I am not lying. For as long as I was healthy I had a very noble lover, now because of her I have these bumps on my skin. She makes me sound these carved clappers night and day and the noise deafens all the people I ask to give me alms for the love of God the Creator.'

'Do not hide anything,' said the king, 'how did your lover give you those bumps?'

'Sir King, her lord was a leper. I had my pleasure with her and this malady came to me from our intercourse. But only one woman is more beautiful than she was.'

'Who is that?'

'The fair Yseut. She dresses the same way as that woman did.'

The king heard this and went off laughing. King Arthur, who had been jousting on the other side, as happy as could be, came up to him and inquired of the queen.

'She is coming through the wood,' said King Mark. 'Sire, she is coming with Andret, it is his task to conduct her here.'

Then they said to each other: 'I do not know how she

will cross this Malpas. Let us stay here and watch out for her.'

The three villains – may they burn in Hell! – came to the ford and asked the leper which way those who were least muddy had passed across. Tristan lifted his crutch and pointed towards a great quagmire.

'You see the peat bog beyond that mud: that is the right direction, I have seen several people pass that way.'

The villains went into the mire where the leper had pointed, but they found the mud was very deep and reached the sides of their saddles. All three fell in, all of a heap. The leper was up on the hill and he shouted:

'Spur your horses if the mud is making you dirty. Come on, sirs! By the Holy Apostle, each of you give me something!'

Their horses sank in the mire and they began to be anxious, for they could not find the bank or firm ground. Those who were jousting on the hill came hurrying down. Now hear how the leper tricked them:

'My lords,' he said to the evil barons, 'hold on to your saddle-bows. A curse on this marsh for being so soft! Take off the cloaks round your necks and move your arms about in the mud. I'm telling you, I know. I've seen lots of people pass through today.'

Who could have imagined how the leper broke his goblet as he shook it and hit the rim with his strap! With his other hand he was shaking his rattle. At that moment the fair Yseut arrived. She saw her enemies in the marsh and her lover sitting on the mound. She was very glad to see this and laughed and felt very cheerful. She dismounted at the bank. The two kings and their barons were on the further side watching the men in the marsh turning on their sides and lying flat as the leper urged them on:

'My lords, the queen has arrived to give her vindication. Go and hear her trial!' And he spoke almost joyfully! Hear how the crippled leper spoke to Denoalan: 'Take hold of my stick and pull hard with both hands.'

The leper quickly held it out to him and he pulled. But the leper let go the stick and the other fell back into the mire until only his hair could be seen standing on end. When he had been pulled out of the mud the leper said:

'I couldn't help it! My joints and muscles are useless, my hands are stiff with disease and my feet are swollen with gout. This malady has made me weak and my arms are withered.'

Dinas was with the queen and saw what was going on. He winked at Tristan, who he well knew was under the cloak. He saw with delight how the three villains were caught in the mire; he was pleased to see them in such a plight. With a great deal of trouble the accusers struggled out of the mire. They would certainly not be clean again without a bath. In front of everyone they stripped and left their old clothes to put on others. But now hear of Dinas who was on the other side of the Malpas. He addressed the queen:

'My lady,' he said, 'your fine cloak is going to be quite spoiled. This marshy ground is full of slime. I am worried that you may get some of it on your clothes.'

Yseut was not afraid, and she smiled at him and winked. Then he realized what the queen had in mind.

He and Andret went a little further down to a ford near a thorn-bush where they crossed over without getting very dirty. Yseut was alone on the other side. Near the ford was the great company of the two kings and their barons. Hear how clever Yseut was. She knew that all those on the other side of Malpas were watching her. She had come on a palfrey, and she tied the straps of the saddle-cloth over the saddle-bow. No squire or servant did any better in keeping them out of the mud or making himself ready to cross. The saddle straps were pushed under the saddle. The fair Yseut unfastened the breast-strap and took the bridle off her palfrey. She was holding her dress in one hand, and in the other she had a whip. She led her palfrey to the ford, struck it with the whip and it crossed over the marsh. The queen was being watched intently by those who were on the other side. The worthy kings were alarmed at what she did next, as were all the others who saw it. The queen was wearing robes of silk brought from Baghdad lined with white ermine. Her cloak and tunic hung down behind her. Her hair fell over her shoulders in a linen headscarf worked with fine gold. She was wearing a gold circlet on her head which showed off her fresh rosy and white colouring. She turned towards the plank bridge and spoke to the leper:

'I want you to do something for me.'

'Kind and noble queen, I come without hesitating but I don't know what you could mean.'

'I do not want my clothes to get muddy. You will be my donkey and carry me carefully across the plank.'

'Ah, noble queen,' he said, 'don't ask me to do this! I am a leper and I am hunch-backed and deformed.'

'Hurry up and make yourself ready,' she said. 'Do you think I will catch your disease? Have no fear, I will not.'

'God,' he said to himself, 'what is going to happen? What a pleasure to talk to her!' He was supporting himself on his crutch.

'Heavens, leper, you are fat! Turn your face that way and your back this way. I will get on like a boy.'

Then the leper smiled and bent his back. The queen mounted. Everyone was watching, kings and counts. Leaning on his crutch he raised one foot and kept the other firmly on the ground. Several times he pretended to fall, and looked as though he was in great pain. The fair Yseut rode on his back with her legs round him. The onlookers said to each other:

'Now look [at that strange sight!] See the queen riding on a leper who is hobbling along. He is almost falling off the plank, holding his crutch on his hip. Let us go to meet the leper when he comes out of the marsh.'

The squires ran [to meet the leper]. King Arthur went over, the others following in their turn. The leper kept his face down as he arrived from the other side. Yseut let herself slide off. The leper prepared to return, and as he was going he asked Yseut for food for that night. Arthur said:

'He has well deserved it, queen, give it to him!'

The fair Yseut said to the king: 'By the faith I owe you, he is a great scoundrel, he has enough. He will not eat today all that he has. I could feel his belt under his cloak. King, his wallet is far from empty: I felt whole loaves, half loaves, pieces of bread and crumbs in his bag.

He has food and he is well clothed. If he wants to sell your gaiters he can get five pieces of silver for them. And with my lord's hood he can buy a good bed and become a shepherd, or buy a donkey to carry him over marshes! As far as I can see, he is a good-for-nothing. He has taken a rich crop here today from the kind of people he likes. He will not get so much as a farthing from me!'

The two kings were much amused. They brought her palfrey to her, helped her to mount and rode away. Those who had arms began to joust. Tristan left that gathering and went back to his squire who was waiting for him. Governal had brought two fine Castilian horses, saddled and bridled, two lances and two shields; he had disguised them well. Of the knights themselves, what shall I say? Governal had put a white silk wrap over his head so that only his eyes could be seen. He backed away slowly on his handsome, well-groomed horse. Tristan was riding Bel Joeor, no better horse could be found. His tunic, saddle, horse and shield were all covered with black serge. A black mask hid his face and he had completely covered his head and body. On his lance he had fixed the token his lady had given him. Each was mounted, with a steel blade at his side. Armed like this on horseback, they passed through a green meadow between two valleys and came into sight of Blanche Lande. Gawain, Arthur's nephew, said to Gerflet:

'Look at those two coming! They are riding very fast. I do not know them. Do you know who they are?'

'I know them well,' replied Gerflet, 'a black horse and a black pennon must belong to the Black Knight of the Mountain. I know the other by his bright arms: there are not many like that in this country. I know beyond doubt that they are enchanted!'

The two knights left the road, their shields held tight, their lances raised with the pennons fastened to the blades. They bore their armour as well as if they had been born inside it. King Arthur and King Mark spoke more of those two knights than they did of all their own companies over on the broad plains. The two knights attracted much attention from the throng and many people were watching them. They spurred together through the outposts but found no one to joust with. The queen knew well who they were; she was standing with Brangain to one side of the knights.

Then Andret came up on horseback, armed. With his lance raised he gripped his shield and aimed directly at Tristan's face. He did not recognize him at all, but Tristan knew Andret, struck him on the shield and unhorsed him in the middle of the track and broke his arm. He lay on his back at the queen's feet without moving. Governal saw coming from the tents on horseback the forester who found Tristan asleep in the forest and tried to send him to his death. Governal went towards him at great speed – surely he was in mortal danger! Governal thrust his sharp blade at the forester's body and the steel pierced his skin. He fell dead, and no priest could ever have come to him in time. The noble and frank Yseut smiled at this under her veil. Gerflet and Cinglor, Yvain, Tolas, Coris and Gawain all saw this defeat of their companions.

'My lords,' said Gawain, 'what shall we do? The forester is lying there with his mouth wide open. Those two are surely enchanted. We have no idea who they are, and now they take us for fools. Let us hasten after them and capture them!'

'Whoever can deliver them to us,' said the king, 'will do us a great service.'

Tristan drew back towards the ford with Governal and they crossed over. The others dared not follow them, they were afraid and stayed where they were. Indeed, they thought the two knights were phantoms. They wanted to make for their lodgings for they had finished jousting. Arthur rode on the queen's right, and their journey seemed to him very short. [The edge of the forest was on their left] and the path continued to the right. They dismounted at their lodgings, of which there were plenty on the heath. Tent-ropes were at a high price. In place of reeds and rushes, they had all carpeted their tents with flowers. By roads and by-ways people came to the Blanche Lande until it was crowded. Many a knight had brought his lover. The knights who were in the meadow found many a stag to pursue. That night they stayed on the heath. Each king sat to hear the requests of his people. Those who were rich were quick to exchange presents. After his meal King Arthur went to the tent of King Mark to pay his respects, taking his private household with him. Little coarse cloth was worn there, almost everything was of silk! Of the clothes what shall I say? There were garments made of the finest wool, dyed scarlet; many people were richly clad. No one ever saw two richer courts. Nothing that they needed was lacking. They made great joy in their tents. That night they discussed the matter in hand, how the queen was to vindicate herself against the accusation in the presence of the kings and their barons. King Arthur went back to his bed with his barons and friends.

Anyone who was in the wood that night could have heard the sounds of flute and shawm coming from the tents. Before daybreak there was thunder, a sure sign of heat. The watchmen sounded their horns at daybreak, and everywhere people woke up and rose without delay. The sun was already hot soon after dawn and the mist and hoar-frost had dispersed. The Cornish people had gathered in front of the tents of the two kings. No knight in the whole kingdom had failed to attend this court with his wife. A cloth of dark grey silk, embroidered with small animal figures, was placed before the king's tent and spread out on the green grass. The cloth had been bought in Nicaea. Not one holy relic was left anywhere in Cornwall in a treasure-chest, in a casket or a phylactery, in reliquaries or boxes or shrines, not even those that were set in gold or silver crosses or amulets, for they had all been placed on the cloth and arranged in their order. The kings drew to one side. They wanted to come to a fair decision. King Arthur, always quick to speak, spoke first:

'King Mark,' he said, 'whoever advised you to make this accusation did you a terrible wrong and certainly acted disloyally. You are easily influenced, but you must not believe false words. The man who made you convene this meeting was preparing a bitter sauce for you. Whoever brought this about deserves to be severely punished. The noble, good Yseut has not asked for any delay. I want those who have come to hear her trial to know this for sure: I will see them hanged if they make any spiteful

accusations of wickedness after her trial. They will
deserve their death. Now listen, King Mark: whoever
is to be proved wrong, let the queen come forward so
that everyone can see her. She shall swear to the Heavenly
King, holding her right hand over the holy relics, that
there was never love between her and your nephew
which was in any way shameful, and that she has never
loved anyone wrongfully. My lord Mark, this has been
going on too long: when Yseut has sworn that oath, tell
your barons to hold their tongues.'

'My lord Arthur, what can I do? You reproach me and
you are right, for only a fool believes an envious man;
yet I believed them against my will. If the queen is
vindicated in this meadow, no one will ever be so bold
again. If anyone, after the trial, speaks of the queen
otherwise than to her honour, he will suffer for it.
Arthur, noble king, know that this has been done
against my will. From now on let them take heed!'

Then the counsellors separated. Everyone sat down
in rows except the two kings, for Yseut was between
them holding their hands. Gawain stood near the relics,
and the household of Arthur was seated round the cloth.
Arthur, who was nearest Yseut, began to speak:

'Listen to me, fair Yseut, and hear what you are
accused of. You must swear that Tristan never loved
you wickedly or wrongfully, and only bore you the love
he owed to his uncle and his wife.'

'My lords,' she said, 'by the mercy of God I see holy
relics here before me. Listen now to what I swear, and
may it reassure the king: so help me God and St Hilary,
and by these relics, this holy place, the relics that are not

141

here and all the relics there are in the world, I swear that no man ever came between my thighs except the leper who carried me on his back across the ford and my husband, King Mark. Those two I exclude from my oath; I exclude no one else in the world. From two men I cannot exculpate myself: the leper and King Mark my lord. The leper was between my legs [as everyone who was watching could see]. If anyone wants me to do more, I am ready here and now.'

All those who heard her oath could bear no more.

'God,' said everyone, 'that would be a cruel wrong! She has done everything that justice demands, and she put more into her oath than the villains required her to. She needs to make no defence concerning the king and his nephew beyond what all of us have already heard. She swore in her oath that no man ever came between her thighs, except the leper who carried her across the ford yesterday morning and King Mark, her husband. A curse on anyone who mistrusts her now!'

King Arthur rose to his feet and addressed King Mark so that all the barons could hear:

'King, we have seen and heard the queen's defence. Now let the three villains Denoalan, Ganelon and the evil Godwin, take care never to speak of it again. As long as they remain in this land, we shall be ready to come swiftly to defend the rights of the fair Queen Yseut as soon as she sends a message.'

'Sire,' she said, 'I thank you.'

The three villains were greatly hated by all the court. The courtiers separated and made their departure. The lovely, fair-haired Yseut thanked King Arthur deeply.

'My lady,' he said, 'I am your surety. As long as I am
alive and healthy, you will never again find that anyone
says anything that is not to your honour. The villains
have had evil thoughts. I have begged the king your
lord, in loyalty and friendship, never to believe what the
villains say about you.'

King Mark said: 'If I do from now on, I shall be
greatly to blame.'

Then they parted from each other and each returned
to his own kingdom. King Arthur went to Durham and
King Mark stayed in Cornwall. Tristan remained where
he was, with few worries.

16

TRISTAN'S VENGEANCE

KING MARK held Cornwall in peace and was feared by
everyone far and near. He wanted Yseut to share in his
pleasures and tried hard to act lovingly towards her.
But, no matter who was at peace, the three villains were
on the watch for more treachery. A spy had come to
them, seeking to improve his fortune.

'My lords,' he said, 'listen to me: if I lie, you can
hang me. The king was angry with you the other day and
began to hate you because of his wife's vindication. You
may hang me or punish me in any way if I cannot
clearly show you Tristan waiting at leisure to talk to his
dear love. He is concealed, but I know his hiding-place.
Tristan knows all about Malpertis! When the king is

going off on a hunting trip he first takes leave of the queen in her room. Now, you can burn me to ashes if you go to her window on the right at the back and do not see Tristan coming in, wearing his sword and holding a bow with a couple of arrows in his other hand. You will be able to see him tonight in the early hours.'

'How do you know?'

'I have seen him.'

'Tristan?'

'Yes, indeed, and I recognized him.'

'When was he there?'

'I saw him there this morning.'

'Who was with him?'

'His friend.'

'His friend? Who?'

'Governal.'

'Where are they staying?'

'They are lodged very comfortably somewhere.'

'At Dinas's house?'

'How should I know?'

'They are not here without his knowledge.'

'That is likely.'

'Where can we see this?'

'Through the bedroom window, I tell you. But if I show you, I must have a lot of money as a reward.'

'How much?'

'A silver mark.'

'You may have more than we promise, so help you Church and Mass. If you show us this you cannot fail to make yourself rich.'

'Now listen,' said the evil spy, 'there is a little narrow

opening just by the queen's bedroom with a curtain hanging in front of it. Beyond the room there is a wide brook where lilies grow thickly: one of you three go there after midnight. Through a gap in the new garden you can easily go up to that opening, but you must not go past the window. Cut a point on the end of a long twig with a sharp knife. Catch the cloth of the curtain with the sharp end of the twig and pull the curtain gently away from the opening – it is not fastened – so that you can see inside clearly when Tristan comes. If you keep watch like that for only three days, then you can burn me if you do not see what I say!'

Each of the three barons said: 'We swear to keep to this agreement.' They sent the spy away. Then they arranged which of the three of them should go first to see the sport that Tristan was enjoying with the woman who was still loyal to him. They agreed that Godwin would go the first time. They parted, each going his own way – tomorrow they would know what Tristan was doing. The noble queen, alas, was not on her guard against the villains and their schemes. She had sent a message to Tristan through her attendant Perinis to come to her next day after midnight, when the king would have gone to St Lubin.

Hear, my lords, the story of what happened. Next day the night was dark. Tristan had made his way through a thicket of thorn bushes. Going out of the copse he looked round and saw Godwin coming out of his hiding place. Tristan waited in ambush, hidden in the thicket.

'God,' he said, 'help me: let the man who is coming not notice me before he is right in front of me!'

He waited, sword in hand, for Godwin, still a long way off. But Godwin went a different way. Tristan stayed where he was, sad to see Godwin going away. Then he left the copse, looking around carefully. But it was useless, for Godwin was increasing the distance, bent on carrying out his evil purpose. Tristan looked further into the distance and had a brief glimpse of Denoalan, who was riding slowly along with two astonishingly big greyhounds. Tristan hid behind an apple-tree. Denoalan came along the path on a small, black palfrey. He had sent his dogs to start a wild boar in the thicket – before they could dislodge it their master was going to receive a blow that no physician could cure! The brave Tristan took off his cloak. Denoalan had soon ridden up, without suspecting anything, and Tristan leaped on him. Denoalan wanted to escape but he could not, for Tristan was too close to him. Tristan killed him. What else could he do, for the other was seeking his death? To save himself he cut off the villain's head and did not even give him the time to say, 'I am wounded.' With his sword he cut off the hair and stuck it in his boots. When he showed Yseut the hair she would know that he had killed the villain. Tristan hurried away from that place.

'Alas,' he said, 'what has become of Godwin? I saw him moving quickly a short while ago and now he has gone. Has he passed me? Did he ride past a moment ago? If he waited for me he would soon find out that he would get no better deserts than the wicked Denoalan – and I left him dead!'

Tristan left the body lying on its back, bleeding, in the middle of the clearing. He cleaned his sword and replaced

it in its sheath. He put on his cloak and pulled the cowl
over his head. He placed a large branch over the body,
then set off to his lover's room. But now hear what
happened to him. Godwin had hurried to the same place
and had arrived before Tristan. He had pushed aside the
curtain and could see the bedroom carpeted with rushes
and everything inside. He could see no man there except
Perinis. Brangain, the maid, came in; she had been
combing Yseut's hair and still had the comb with her.
The villain at the wall saw Tristan come in holding a
bow of tough laburnum wood with two arrows in one
hand, and in the other some long tresses. He took off his
cloak, revealing his well-made body. The lovely, fair-
haired Yseut rose to greet him. At her window she caught
sight of the shadow of Godwin's head. The queen was
quick to see this, and it made her sweat with fear. Tristan
said to her:

'God keeps me amongst His own! This is Denoalan's
hair, I have avenged you on him. Never again will he
buy a sword or lance and use them!'

'My lord,' she said, 'what am I to do? I beg you to
stretch this bow and we shall see how it is bent.'

Tristan bent the bow, thinking to himself. He thought
hard, realized her meaning and drew his bow. He asked
for news of King Mark and Yseut told him all she knew.
[Godwin was watching them with evil thoughts in his
mind.] If he had escaped alive, he would have made war
to the death on King Mark and his wife Yseut; but the
man to whom God granted honour would take care that
he did not escape. Yseut had no wish to talk.

'My love, fit an arrow to the string and take care that

the string is not twisted. I can see something that troubles me.'

Tristan stood still and thought for a moment. He realized that she could see something that had displeased her. He looked up and trembled with fear: against the light by the curtain he saw Godwin's head.

'God, our true King, I have had many fine shots with bow and arrow: grant me not to miss with this one! I can see one of the three Cornish villains standing outside there. God, who allowed Your Own most holy body to suffer death for your people's sake, let me avenge myself on these villains for all the wrong they have done me!'

Then he turned to the wall. The bow had many times been bent, and now he shot. The arrow flew so fast that nothing could have escaped it. It pierced Godwin's eye and went deep into his head and his brain. No hawks or swallows could fly with half the speed of that arrow; it would not have gone more easily into a soft apple. He fell and struck a post; he lay without moving hand or foot. He was not even able to say, 'I am wounded. God, confession!'

Yseut then said to Tristan:

'*You must flee for your own safety! All the villains are now dead, but your hiding-place is known and your life is in danger if you remain here.*'

So the lovers took a sorrowful farewell of each other and renewed their exchange of love tokens. Each promised to be always at the service of the other.

17

TRISTAN IN BRITTANY

*Tristan left with Governal to seek adventure in foreign lands.
After travelling for some time they came to Brittany, to the
land of Duke Hoel. The duke was engaged at that time in
defending his land against hostile invaders and Tristan
promptly offered his services. The duke gratefully accepted
and, with Tristan's help, succeeded in driving off the enemy.
Tristan became friendly with Hoel's son, Kaherdin, and
daughter, Yseut of the White Hands. But he continued to
yearn for Yseut the Fair in Cornwall, and sang a number of
sad lays about her. Kaherdin overheard Tristan singing of
his love for Yseut, and mistakenly thought the affection was
for his sister. Kaherdin told his father, and Hoel was
delighted and offered Tristan his daughter Yseut in marriage.
After much deliberation Tristan accepted this offer, thinking
he would never see Yseut the Fair again and, moreover,
being greatly pleased by the name as well as the beauty of
Yseut of the White Hands. The marriage took place. On the
wedding night, however, Tristan was suddenly reminded of
Yseut the Fair when he caught sight of the ring she gave him
when they parted. At once he began to regret his marriage
and, although he lay in the same bed with his bride, he left the
marriage unconsummated, explaining that he was in great
pain from an old wound.*

*Yseut of the White Hands accepted this situation for
some time, until one day she was out riding with her brother
and her horse went through some water which splashed her*

thighs. Yseut laughed, and accused the water of being bolder than any man had ever been. The astonished Kaherdin questioned her and learned the truth about her marriage. As soon as he could, Kaherdin angrily reproached Tristan with what he regarded as an insult to his family. In reply, Tristan told Kaherdin of his love for Yseut the Fair who was, he said, even more beautiful than Kaherdin's sister. To convince Kaherdin of the truth of Tristan's words, the two men set out on a voyage to Cornwall.

They learned that Mark's court was due to pass along a certain road and lay in hiding close by the side of the road. As the procession came into sight, Kaherdin was overcome by the magnificent display and especially by the great beauty of all the ladies. Tristan succeeded in passing a message to Yseut the Fair who contrived to spend the night in a nearby castle, where she welcomed Tristan and Kaherdin. She reproached Tristan for his marriage, of which news had reached her, but soon forgave him and their old love was renewed. It was too dangerous for Tristan to remain long in Cornwall, and he and Kaherdin soon returned to Brittany, once again firm friends.

Tristan continued to languish for his beloved. He dared not return to Cornwall because of all the harm he had done to King Mark.

18

TRISTAN'S MADNESS

TRISTAN lived at court in a state of confusion, for he could not think what to do. He greatly feared King Mark, for Mark had threatened him harshly: he wanted Tristan to know that if he could get Tristan in his power neither Tristan's blood nor his lineage would save him from being put to death. He had wronged Mark through his wife. Mark laid a formal complaint before his barons about the shame and the scandal that Tristan had caused him. He was ashamed of what Tristan had done, for it could no longer be concealed. He called all his barons together to tell them what had happened, and he revealed all Tristan's wrongdoing.

'My lords,' he said, 'what can I do? I am deeply vexed that I did not take vengeance on Tristan, and I am being called a fool for this. He has fled from this land and I do not know where to search for him. By St Andrew, I should greatly regret it if Tristan were now forever safe from my vengeance. If any of you can find out where he is, let me know without delay. By St Samson of Cornwall, if anyone could give him up to me I should be greatly pleased and I should always love him!'

There was not one of his barons who did not promise to make efforts to capture Tristan. Dinas the Seneschal sighed; for Tristan's sake he felt angry, and he was much grieved by Mark's threats. Hastily he sent a message to Tristan to tell him that through his folly he had forfeited the love of the king, who now bore him mortal hatred. The pleasures Tristan had enjoyed had turned out badly: he had been spied on by jealous people and betrayed.

When Tristan heard this news you may know that he was far from pleased. He dared not return to the country where for so long he lived as a fugitive. He sighed many times and lamented bitterly that Yseut was not with him. There was an Yseut with him, but not she who was his first love. He thought hard about what to do and how he could persuade his love to come to him, since he dared not go to her country.

'Oh, God,' he said, 'what a fate! What I have suffered for the sake of love! I never complained of my love, nor do I now lament of my distress. But why does love assail me? Why wound me? God, what should I do? [For it seems to me that I have already suffered greatly because of my love.] Have I not done all that love requires? No, for I have abandoned the woman who suffered so much shame and hardship for my sake! Alas, how unhappy I am – I was indeed born in an unlucky hour! [And Yseut, too, for my sake] has endured so much distress. No one ever saw such a beautiful woman! A man who grows weary of loving her is not worthy of being loved himself and deserves to be called faint-hearted. May love, which conquers all things, grant me my desire to hold her once more in my arms. Surely I shall do so, if it please God. I pray God not to let me die before I have her again. She skilfully healed the wound that I received in Cornwall, when I swam to an island to fight against Morholt to prevent him from claiming the tribute owed by the Cornish people. My sword ended that battle. God grant

that I may live long enough to see her safe and sound! It
would still give me great joy to be re-united with her.
May God in His mercy give her health and happiness,
if it please Him. And may He grant me joy and honour,
and let me find a way to reach her and see her again. God,
how I am humbled, and how little respected in that land!
Alas, what shall I do if I cannot see her? Because of her
I am in great agitation at every moment of the night and
day. When I do not see her I nearly go out of my mind.
Alas, what shall I do? I cannot think what to do, I am
so upset because of her. She might think me a coward if
threats were enough to stop me; for I could always go to
her in secret or dressed like some pitiable madman. For
her sake I am willing to be shaven and shorn if I cannot
disguise myself any other way. I am too well known in
that country, I should be found out straight away unless
I altered my clothes and my appearance sufficiently. I
shall not cease my journey to find her while I can still go
one step further!'

When that idea occurred to him he did not delay and
started off that very instant, leaving behind his country
and his kingdom. He took with him neither hauberk nor
helmet. He went on walking night and day and did not
stop until he reached the sea. Only with great difficulty
did he walk so far; and I can tell you that he had suffered
such hardships for her that indeed he was already a
madman. He changed his name and called himself
Tantris.

When he had crossed the sea and arrived in Cornwall
he quickly went away from the shore. He did not want
anyone to think he was in his senses and he tore his

clothes and scratched his face. He struck any man who crossed his path. He had his fair hair shorn off. Nobody on the seashore thought he was anything but mad, for they did not know what was in his mind. He was carrying a staff in his hand. He walked along looking like a fool and everyone shouted after him and threw stones at his head. Tristan went on without stopping. He walked like this through the land for many days, all for love of Yseut. Whatever he did seemed good to him, and nothing displeased him except that he was not with Yseut: he desired her and longed for her. He had not yet been to the court, but now he was going, whatever the outcome. He would make himself appear to be a fool, for he wanted to speak to Yseut.

He was able to walk straight into the court, for no door was closed to the fool. When Tristan presented himself before the king, his appearance was somewhat unprepossessing: with short-cropped hair and a long neck he looked remarkably like a fool. He had taken great trouble, all for the sake of love. Mark called to him and asked:

'Fool, what is your name?'

'My name is Picous.'

'Who was your father?'

'A walrus.'

'By whom did he have you?'

'A whale. I have a sister I will bring to you. The girl is called Bruneheut: you shall have her and I will have Yseut.'

'If we exchange, what will you do?'

'Listen to this!' said Tristan. 'Between the clouds and

the sky, where there is no frost, I shall build a house of
flowers and roses and there she and I will enjoy ourselves.
I have not yet finished the story I am telling these Welsh-
men – may God shame them! King Mark, the maiden
Brangain – with my hand in yours I assure you this is true
– gave Tristan the drink which caused him such distress
afterwards. I can see Yseut over there: she and I drank
it – ask her! And if she says that is a lie, then I say it is a
lie that I have dreamed every night since! Even now, king,
there is more to tell. Look me straight in the face: do I
not look like Tantris? I have leaped and thrown reeds
and balanced sharpened twigs,[4] I have lived on roots in
a wood and I have held a queen in my arms. I shall say
more if I have a mind to.'

'Rest yourself now, Picolet. I am sorry you have done
so many things. Leave your jesting for today.'

'What does it matter to me if you are sorry? I do not
care a scrap!'

Then all the knights said: 'No one heeds a fool or
argues with him.'

'Do you remember your great fear when you found us
lying in the bower with my naked sword between us?[5] I
pretended to be asleep then, for I dared not escape. It
was warm then, as it is in May. There was a ray of sun-
light coming through the leaves, shining on her face.
God's will was done. You pushed your gloves into a gap
in the branches and went away. Nothing else happened;
nor do I want to go on talking, for he ought to remember
it well.'

Mark looked at the queen, who was keeping her head
bowed and had covered her face with her cloak.

'Fool, a curse on the sailors who brought you across the sea and did not throw you into the water!'

Tristan answered: 'My lady, a curse on your fool! If you were sure who I was, if you were alone with me and found out all about me, then no door or barred window nor any king's command would keep you away from me. I still have with me the ring you gave me when we parted from each other at that meeting with King Mark which I have hated ever since. A curse on that meeting! I had many a hard day to suffer afterwards. Make up for the loss, my lady, with sweet kisses of true love or embraces beneath the sheets. I am sure you could give me great comfort or I should die. Never did Yder, who killed the bear, suffer such hardships for Arthur's wife, Guinevere,[6] as I do for you, for I am dying of them. Because of this I left behind the whole of Brittany; I went to Spain on my own – my friends never knew this, nor did Kaherdin's sister. I wandered far by land and sea until I came here in search of you. If I go away now, if there is no feeling inside you, then I have lost all hope of joy. Let no one ever believe in prophecies!'

Many people were whispering to each other in the hall: 'In my opinion, the king would soon come to believe this fool!'

King Mark then called for horses; he wanted to go out to watch his birds, which were not long out of moult, flying after the cranes. Everyone went out and the hall was left empty. Tristan leaned on a bench. The queen went into her own marble-floored room and called her maid:

'By St Christine, have you heard the amazing things that fool is saying? May he get palsy in his ears! He reminded me today of many things that I did with Tristan, whom I have loved so much and still do without any pretence. Alas, the fool despises me, yet I cannot bring myself to send him away. Go and bring the fool to me.'

The maid went out quickly. Tristan was very pleased to see her.

'Sir fool, my lady is asking for you. You have taken some trouble today to recount the story of her life. You are full of mischief. So help me God, anyone who hanged you would be doing a good deed!'

'No, Brangain, he certainly would not: there are bigger fools than me on horseback.'

'What enchanters can have told you my name?'

'Fair Brangain, I have known it for a long time. By this head of mine, which was once fair, this fool has lost his reason and it is your fault. This very day I am going to ask you as a recompense to help me in getting the queen to give me a fair reward for only a quarter of my service to her, or for a half of my suffering.'

Then he heaved a great sigh. Brangain had been watching him closely. She could see that he had extremely well-made arms, hands and feet, and a shapely waist. In her heart she thought that he was sensible and that what was ailing him was something nobler than lunacy.

'Sir knight, may God give you honour and joy. But let nothing happen which could turn to the queen's dishonour nor to mine, for I am among her friends. Forgive me for what I said – I am more than a little sorry for it.'

'I forgive you, it doesn't trouble me.'

Then Brangain said kindly: 'Please go on, whatever you are trying to do, but take some other name than Tristan.'

'Indeed, I gladly would! But the potion which you found in the chest has so robbed me of my reason and my will-power that I have no thoughts beyond obeying the dictates of love. God grant it will come to a happy end! Woe that this was all begun, for my good sense has indeed changed to madness. Brangain, you surely did us a bad turn when you brought us the potion. Many different herbs were mixed in the brew and it is affecting us unequally, for I am dying for her while she does not feel it. Our fate is unjustly shared, and I am the ill-starred Tristan.'

At those words Brangain knew who he was. She fell at his feet asking for forgiveness and begging him to pardon her for her cruelty. He took her hand, made her rise and kissed her many times. Then he asked her to help him in his task without more delay, for she could easily tell Yseut; he asked her to do all she could. Brangain took his hand and held him close to her side as she led the way into Yseut's room. Yseut saw the fool and her heart beat faster because she hated him for the rash words he had spoken that morning. He greeted her politely and without flattery, not knowing how things would turn out.

'God save the queen,' he said, 'and Brangain her maid. She could soon cure my sickness just by calling me her love. I am a lover, so is she. Our love is not equally divided: I suffer doubly, but she has no pity for me. I have suffered many hardships, hunger and thirst, rough places to sleep, and the deep grief that I bear in my heart. No one could reproach me with being idle. But I pray to God – who at the wedding of Cana was such a pleasant steward that he changed the water into wine! – may God inspire her to rid me of this madness.'

Yseut kept her peace and said not a word. Brangain saw this and said to her:

'My lady, what sort of welcome is this to give to the truest lover that ever was or ever will be? He is tormented by his love for you. Put your arms around his neck quickly! It is because of you that his hair has been shorn off like a madman. My lady, listen to what I am saying: this is Tristan, I assure you!'

'Maid, you are wrong. I wish you and he were both far away in the port where he arrived this morning. This young man is too sly. If he were Tristan, he would not have said such awful things about me today in front of everyone in the hall – he would have done better to stay in the hold of his ship!'

'My lady, I did that to keep our secret and to make fools of them all. Formerly I knew nothing of this sort of deception, but love for you drives me to it. You do not remember Gamarien, who demanded nothing less than your person and abducted you: who was it who delivered you from him?'

'That was certainly the king's nephew, Tristan. He was a handsome knight.'

Tristan heard this and it pleased him, for he knew that she would give him her love, and he asked no more. He had been in great distress because of his love.

'Do I not look like the man who came to you alone and without assistance when you needed help, and cut off Gamarien's hand?'[7]

'Yes, insofar as you are a man. I do not know you, and there is an end to it.'

'That is very sad, my lady. I was once your harpist[8] and played to you in your room at a time when I was very sorrowful, and you were yourself a little sad. The wound I had which he gave me through the shoulder – that was how I left the battle – you cured and brought me back to health. Yours was the only hand that touched me. You cured me, too, of the poison from the horrible dragon – may I be hanged if I lie! And when I was in the bath you took out my sword and found the notch as you cleaned the blade. Then you called Perinis to bring the piece of dark silk the splinter was wrapped in. You joined the splinter to the sword and when you saw that it fitted you did not love me at all! In your wrath you grasped the sword in both hands to strike me and came towards me angrily. But I soon calmed you by telling you the story of the golden hair, which has since caused me such sorrow. Your mother knew this secret, I assure you in good faith. Then you were entrusted to my care. On the third day after we left port the wind dropped. We all had to take the oars and I myself lent a hand.[9] It was very hot and we were thirsty. Brangain, who is before you now, hurried to the cupboard but she made a mistake in what she was looking for: she filled a cup with the love potion. It looked like clear wine and you could not see that there was anything mixed with it. She brought it to me and I took it. It did you little harm then or afterwards, but you know well enough what happened. It was unlucky for me that I ever saw you, damsel!'

'You have certainly had a good teacher. Now you want us to think you are Tristan, God save him! But we can easily get rid of you. Have you more to tell us?'

'Yes: the leap from the chapel. When you were condemned to be burnt and then handed over to the lepers, they went along quarrelling and disputing which of them should have you in the wood until the choice fell on one. I was waiting in ambush, alone except for Governal. You certainly ought to know me, for I broke many heads that day – or rather none of them was harmed by me, but Governal – God save him! – gave them great blows with the sticks they used as crutches. Then we were in the forest for a while, and we shed many a tear there. Is the hermit Ogrin still alive? God rest his soul!'

'Leave that alone! It is not your place to speak of him. You are not at all like Tristan: he is a fine man and you are a wretch. You have taken on a strange task – beggary makes you deceitful. I could very soon have you taken prisoner and let the king hear all about what you have done.'

'If he knew that, my lady, I am sure you would be very sad. They say "whoever serves love will one day be rewarded for everything." From what I have seen here, this is not true in my case. Once I had a lover, indeed, but it seems to me now that I have lost her.'

'Who has caused you that sorrow, sir?'

'She who has loved me for so long and who will yet love me, please God! She must not abandon me now. I

will tell you something else: a dog has a strange nature.
Now, what has become of Husdant? They kept him
tied up for three days, and he refused to eat or drink.
He went mad because of me. Then they broke the dog's
chains and opened the door of his kennel. He ran with-
out stopping straight to me, I assure you by the faith I
owe you.'

'Certainly, the dog is in my safe-keeping for the sake
of his master, for I hope that one day we shall be happy
together again.'

'For me that dog would leave the fair Yseut. Show him
to me straight away to see if he will recognize me.'

'Recognize! A rash thing to say! Since Tristan left no
man has ever approached him that he did not try to bite,
and he will make no allowances for all your wretched-
ness. He is whining in the room over there. Bring him
here, damsel.'

Brangain ran to untie him. When the dog heard
Tristan's voice he pulled the leash out of the maid's
hands, straining to get to Tristan. He leaped on him and
pushed his head back – never was an animal so happy!
He nuzzled Tristan and pawed the ground for joy: any-
one who saw it would have been greatly moved. He
licked his hands and barked gleefully. Yseut was utterly
amazed when she saw this and feared the fool might be
some enchanter or magician. Tristan had poor clothing.
He spoke to the dog:

'I bless the food I gave you! You have not lost your
affection for me. You have given me a much better
reception than the woman I loved so much. She still
thinks I am pretending. But she shall see now the proof

that I am telling the truth: when we parted sorrowfully from each other she kissed me and gave me this little gold ring. I have always carried it with me. Many a time I have spoken to it, hoping to be consoled; and when there was no reply I felt I should die of grief. For love I would kiss the emerald, and my eyes would be wet with hot tears.'

Yseut recognized the ring and saw how the dog was nearly mad with joy. Then she knew in her heart that she was speaking to Tristan.

'Alas,' she said, 'I must be insane! Oh my wicked heart, why do you not break when you do not know the man who has suffered most for me in all the world? Forgive me, my lord. I repent.'

She fell in a swoon and he caught her. Now Brangain could see what she had wanted. When Yseut came to herself she put her arms around him and kissed his eyes and nose and face countless times.

'Tristan, my lord, it is terrible that you are suffering such hardships for me! I am no daughter of a king if I do not give you your reward now. Now, Brangain, what shall it be?'

'My lady, do not make a joke of it. Go and find clothes for him. He is Tristan and you are Yseut. Now we can see that the person who complains the most has the least occasion to!'

Yseut said: 'What comfort can we give him?'

'As long as you have the time, do all you can to please him until Mark comes back from the river.'

'May he find so many fish that he does not come back for a week!'

When Yseut had said this, as you have heard it related here, Tristan slipped under the sheets without another word and held the queen in his arms.

But Tristan could not remain long in Cornwall without discovery and once again he returned to Brittany and Yseut of the White Hands. But he still longed for Yseut the Fair.

19

THE DEATH OF THE LOVERS

Tristan helped his friend Kaherdin in carrying on a love affair with the wife of a neighbouring knight. One day as they were leaving the knight's castle they were attacked by the retainers of the angry knight, who had discovered their activities. Kaherdin was killed and Tristan badly wounded. Yseut of the White Hands had Tristan brought back to the palace where she summoned physicians to attend to his wounds. But his greatest pain was beyond the skill of those physicians; it came from a poisoned wound, and he knew that only Yseut the Fair could cure it. He decided accordingly to send a messenger to her: he was to show her the ring she had given Tristan and beg her to come to Brittany to see him. If the messenger was successful in his mission, his ship was to bear white sails on his return; if not, black sails. The messenger went to Cornwall as quickly as he could and found his way to Yseut the Fair. He identified himself by means of the ring and gave her his message. Without a moment's delay, Yseut set out with the messenger to come to Tristan.

Tristan's health was daily becoming worse, and he was no

longer able to leave his bed. When news came that the ship with his messenger was in sight, he asked his wife anxiously what colour the sails were. But Yseut of the White Hands had overheard Tristan's instructions to his messenger, and out of jealousy she told him falsely that the sails were black. Believing that at the last his beloved Yseut had failed him, Tristan fell back on his bed and died. When Yseut landed, the lamentation and grief of the people of Brittany told her of the death of Tristan. She hurried, griefstricken, to the palace where he lay, kissed him and died as she held him in her arms.

The bodies were taken to Cornwall, for King Mark had decided to give them an honourable burial in the church of Tintagel, one on each side of the nave. The story is told of two trees that grew miraculously, one from Tristan's tomb and one from Yseut's; their branches intertwined over the apse. Three times King Mark had the trees cut down, and three times they grew again. Some say it was the power of the love potion that did this.

NOTES

1. Mark is here confusing two separate episodes: Tristan's suffering at sea was caused by the poisoned wound from Morholt's sword, whereas the wound Tristan received from the dragon was cured by Yseut in Ireland.

2. The text of the manuscript is obscure at this unfortunately crucial point. I have accepted the emendation proposed by E. Muret in his edition of the text, *Roman de Tristan par Beroul* (Paris, 4th edition, 1962).

3. This allusion is far from clear: it does not apparently refer to anything in Beroul's poem. A possible analogue which has been suggested is an episode in the *Tristan* poem by Eilhart von Oberg, which takes place when King Arthur and his knights and Tristan are all at King Mark's court. The jealous Mark places sharp blades round Yseut's bed so that Tristan would be wounded if he should go to her. The trap works and Tristan is wounded, but to help Tristan out of his difficulty all Arthur's knights wound themselves likewise.

4. The reference to the normal accomplishments of a fool recalls at the same time two of Tristan's exploits: his leap from the chapel; and the twigs thrown into the stream to signify to Yseut his presence in the orchard.

5. An allusion which does not accord with what actually happened when King Mark found the lovers, for the king felt no fear (p. 92). But the allusion accurately recalls Tristan's mistaken analysis of the king's actions (p. 95).

6. Yder is a little-known Celtic hero who makes a brief appearance in the Arthurian cycle as the lover of Guinevere, a role traditionally assigned to Lancelot.

7. Presumably an allusion to the episode of 'The Harp and the Rote' (p. 46, summary), although the name Gamarien appears in no other romance. The details of the original version of

Yseut's abduction are not known with certainty and it is possible that it ended with a combat, as implied here. On the other hand, this may be a confusion with Tristan's combat with Morholt, for in Eilhart's poem Tristan cut off his adversary's hand.

8. An allusion to Tristan's first stay in Ireland, when Yseut healed the wound he had received from Morholt and he taught her to play the harp.

9. A detail also given only by the fourteenth-century English poem *Sir Tristrem*.

INDEX OF NAMES

The lists of page references following each entry are not exhaustive.

INDEX OF NAMES

PENGUIN ONLINE